Islam

Islam

What Non-Muslims Should Know

John Kaltner

Fortress Press
Minneapolis

ISLAM
What Non-Muslims Should Know

Translations from the Arabic are the author's.

Cover image: Iran. Isfahan. Friday Mosque. The Oljeitu Mihrab. 1310. / Photo © Tarker / Bridgeman Images
Cover design: Laurie Ingram

Library of Congress Cataloging-in-Publication Data
Print ISBN: 978-1-5064-1666-3
eBook ISBN: 978-1-5064-1667-0

The paper used in this publication meets the minimum requirements of American National Standard for Information Sciences — Permanence of Paper for Printed Library Materials, ANSI Z329.48-1984.

Manufactured in the U.S.A.

This book was produced using Pressbooks.com, and PDF rendering was done by PrinceXML.

To the members of the Memphis Islamic Center

Theirs is an abode of peace from their Lord.

He is their friend because of what they have done.

—Qur'an 6:127

Contents

Contents

Preface

Islam has been at the center of many events and developments throughout the world since its emergence more than fourteen hundred years ago. In the past several decades alone, it has exerted tremendous influence in the political, social, economic, and spiritual arenas, to name but a few. As the fastest-growing religion in the world, Islam attracts new followers every day, and there is every reason to assume that it will continue to play a leading role on the world stage. It is therefore very important for non-Muslims to know as much as they can about this significant and often misunderstood faith.

The aim of this book is to introduce non-Muslims to the basics of Islam so that they will be encouraged to expand and develop their knowledge of it. The space limitations of this work make a comprehensive introduction to the religion impossible. The six aspects of Islam that are discussed here are central to the faith, and familiarity with them will form a solid foundation upon which to build a more complete understanding of the religion. The list of recommended resources at the end suggests some books and other aids that will facilitate further study of Islam.

The first edition of this book was written in the shadow of the tragic events that occurred on September 11, 2001, when I was invited to speak to many congregations and organizations whose members sought to understand the possible motivations and causes behind the attacks that took place that day. In the intervening years, many non-Muslims have become better informed about Islam, and that might be the one silver lining that can be found within the enormous cloud that was 9/11. Despite this increased awareness on the part of some, though, there are regular reminders that others remain in the dark about the essentials of the religion or rely on misinformation that perpetuates stereotypes and impedes good relations with Muslims. Only a few of these people grab headlines and become the subjects of discussion and debate, like preachers who wish to burn the Qur'an and politicians who want to ban all Muslims from entering their country. Others are out of the spotlight and remain anonymous, but their distorted impressions of Muslims and Islam can leave their mark nonetheless, and so the work of educating ourselves remains a high priority.

The group to whom this book is dedicated deserves special mention. The Memphis Islamic Center has been tireless and creative in its efforts to improve relations among people of different religious traditions. Its members have hosted and supported many gatherings that have put Muslims and non-Muslims in conversation with one another in ways that have enhanced mutual understanding and respect. I am proud to call them my friends.

The Qur'an translations used throughout this book are my own. An abbreviated version of this material first appeared in the Winter 2002 issue of *Rhodes Magazine*. I thank former editor Martha Shepard and the staff of the magazine for their fine work on that article. I also wish to express my gratitude to Fortress Press, particularly Michael West for supporting the first edition of this book, and Will Bergkamp for his assistance with this revised edition. A final word of thanks goes to Debra Bartelli for the encouragement and advice she offered while I wrote and revised this book.

1

Islam Is a Diverse and Complex Faith

Difference of opinion within my community is a sign of the bounty of Allah.
—The Prophet Muhammad

No religion in recent times has labored under more stereotypes than Islam. Ask a non-Muslim for a description of the "typical" Muslim, and he or she will probably respond with one or more stock characterizations, the most common being a veiled woman, a bearded cleric, a desert dweller, and a suicide bomber. If you were to inquire further and ask for practices with which Islam is associated, the list would undoubtedly include such things as polygamy, amputation of limbs, terrorist activities, and anti-Western demonstrations.

What impact do such images and impressions have on non-Muslims? What influence do they exert on attitudes toward Muslims and their faith? The answer to these questions depends on how familiar one is with Islam and its followers. Those who have some understanding of the religion will be able to recognize each of the above responses for what it is: just one manifestation or aspect of Islam. Others, especially those with a less firm grasp of the facts, run a certain risk. They need to avoid the temptation to generalize and therefore see the veiled woman or the suicide bomber as representing *the* face of Islam, and terrorism as something all Muslims support.

The first thing non-Muslims should know about Islam is that it is a diverse and complex faith. It can be difficult to recognize this fact because we are often presented with a monochromatic and one-dimensional view of the faith. Most of us rely on the news media to get our information about Islam, but the time and space limitations of news coverage rarely allow for the type of in-depth treatment needed to adequately contextualize a story that is related to this complex faith. A further problem is the issue of media bias. Objective reporting about Islam often falls victim to political and personal agendas that can distort the facts and obscure the truth.

Another factor that should not be underestimated is the role that Hollywood and the entertainment industry sometimes plays in shaping impressions of Islam and its adherents. Television and film portrayals often tap into and perpetuate certain stereotypes about Muslims by making them "come alive." The experience of seeing one's archetype Muslim on the screen in living color can often be an affirmation of its authenticity, even if it is based on a cliché or a misperception.

The simple facts argue against the construction of such a

shallow view of Islam. There are currently more than one and one-half billion Muslims in the world—nearly one-quarter of the population of the planet—and they are found in every part of the globe. It would be foolish to believe that all of these people think and behave exactly the same way. While all Muslims share certain beliefs and practices, there is a rich diversity to the faith. Many of these differences are inconsequential, but others have profound implications. This chapter will explore the issue of the diversity of the Islamic community.

EARLY YEARS

The saying, or *ḥadīth*, from the Prophet Muhammad (570–632) found at the beginning of this chapter indicates that difference within the early Islamic community was not only encouraged, but valued as a sign of divine favor. The circumstances of Muhammad's life made him keenly aware of the presence of difference and the potential it held for both uniting and dividing people. He was born in Mecca, a city in the western portion of modern-day Saudi Arabia that continues to be the center of the Islamic faith. At about the age of forty, he had the first of what he and his followers determined to be a series of revelations from Allah (an Arabic term that translates literally as "the God"). These revelations continued intermittently throughout the remainder of his life and, according to Muslim belief, they are faithfully recorded in Islam's sacred text, the Qur'an (literally, "the recitation").

The primary message Muhammad communicated to his contemporaries was a simple one: Allah is the one true God to whose will all people should submit. It is this idea that gave the religion its name—the Arabic word *islām* means "submission." This message was not attractive to the people of Mecca, particularly its leaders. Their city was an important religious site that housed the *ka'bah*, a shrine associated with numerous gods that was a destination for the many pilgrims who traveled to Mecca each year. Muslim tradition says 360 different deities were worshipped in Mecca, so Muhammad's claim that Allah was the one God posed a clear threat to the Meccan religious system. In addition, acceptance of Islam would have had a negative impact on the local economy since the pilgrims who frequented the city were a major source of revenue. Ironically, after the emergence of Islam Mecca continued to thrive as a pilgrimage site despite the concerns of some of Muhammad's contemporaries. Each year millions of Muslims visit the city to participate in the annual pilgrimage rituals and circumambulate the *ka'bah*, which became a site associated with monotheism during Muhammad's lifetime.

Despite these obstacles, Muhammad was able to attract a small group of converts from among the Meccans, but the Islamic sources indicate that his appeal to reject polytheism fell mostly on deaf ears. His fortunes turned when he was invited to serve as a judge for the people of Yathrib, a town some 200 miles north of Mecca. In the year 622 Muhammad and a small band of his followers made the trip to Yathrib and began to establish a Muslim presence in that part of the Arabian peninsula. This event, the *hijrah* (an Arabic term meaning "migration"), is considered to be the official beginning of the Muslim community, and it was of such historic importance that it marked the starting point of the Islamic calendar. Muhammad spent the last ten years of his life in Yathrib, and it quickly became Islam's operational center. His association with the city was so strong that its name was changed to *madīnat al-nabī* ("the city of the prophet"), and it is known as Medina (also spelled Madina) to this day.

One of the most interesting things about Yathrib was the relatively large number of Jewish people living in the area. This was different from the situation in Mecca, where there was less Jewish or Christian presence. In Yathrib, several of the most prominent tribes for whom Muhammad served as a judge were predominantly Jewish and therefore already monotheists. Consequently, they enjoyed a special relationship with the Muslim community that was not possible for the polytheists of Yathrib. This distinction comes out clearly in a document known as the "Constitution of Medina," which goes back to Muhammad's time and lays down the rules for how the various groups in the area should relate among themselves. The Constitution of Medina makes it clear that the Jews of Yathrib were allowed to maintain their religious identity and that they would be protected by Muhammad's followers. One section reads, "Believers are allies to each other to the exclusion of other people. Help and equality shall be given to the Jews who follow us. They shall not suffer injustice nor shall their enemies be aided." Jews were not the only monotheists who enjoyed a special relationship with Muslims during the early days of Islam. In 630, about two years before his death, Muhammad established a pact with the Christians of Najran, an important center of Christianity in southern Arabia, that guaranteed them protection and freedom of worship.

The issue of the relationship between Islam and the other monotheistic religions will be treated in a later chapter. For now, it is important to note that Muhammad understood himself to be somehow aligned with those earlier faiths while correcting the errors that had crept into them. This means he made efforts to do all he could to attract his fellow monotheists to Islam and invite them to join his growing community. This concern is seen in a number of ways. While all Muslims today turn toward Mecca to pray five times a day, Muhammad originally had his followers turn toward Jerusalem, just as the Jews of Arabia did when they prayed. According to some traditions, he also encouraged the early Muslims to fast during the Jewish feast of Yom Kippur. Similarly, many of the practices of Islam, like prayer, fasting, professing one's faith, and pilgrimage had equivalents within the other monotheistic faiths. Islam therefore had an air of familiarity that would have been attractive to those whose faiths shared similar aspects. The presence of stories in the Qur'an that have clear biblical parallels (a phenomenon discussed below) also functioned in the same way.

Muhammad enjoyed some success in convincing Jews and others in Medina to embrace Islam, but there were problems. Soon after he arrived in Yathrib, tensions between the Jewish tribes and the newly arrived Muslims began to surface and they occasionally reached the boiling point. According to his biography, on several occasions Muhammad felt he had been betrayed by the Jews, and there were several armed conflicts between his followers and Jewish forces. Beyond this was the question of Mecca and how to incorporate it into the Muslim fold. A number of military encounters and raids that pitted the early Muslim community against Meccans figure prominently in Islamic sources, and several of them are mentioned in the Qur'an. While each side had its share of victories and defeats, these experiences helped to bolster the confidence of the nascent Muslim nation.

The early Islamic community sometimes had to resort to violence, but this should not be taken by non-Muslims as an indication that Islam is by nature a violent and aggressive faith. Muhammad and his first followers occasionally found themselves in precarious situations that required them to take the offensive in order to survive. At times, powerful factions and groups were pitted against them, and the Muslims could only rely on each other and their own wits to overcome these obstacles. In their early stages, small and vulnerable movements often have to respond aggressively to perceived threats, and that was the case for Muhammad and his followers at the outset. Once Islam became an established faith it was no longer necessary to adopt such measures to ensure its survival and growth.

Toward the end of his life, Muhammad attempted to win over Mecca to Islam, and he was ultimately successful with a peaceful takeover of the city in the year 630. The description of his triumphant reentry into his hometown and his destruction of the idols contained in the *ka'bah* is one of the most celebrated events of his life for Muslims. At the time of his death two years later, virtually all of the western section of the Arabian peninsula had been converted to Islam.

This brief summary of the founding of Islam shows that the Muslim community was a diverse and complex one from the very beginning. The population from which the first Muslims were drawn was anything but a monolithic or homogeneous entity. Some, like Muhammad himself, were born and raised as polytheists who followed the form of religion prevalent in that time and area. Joining Islam required that they reject the faith of their ancestors and contemporaries, leave behind their familiar gods and goddesses, and become monotheists. Some of them undoubtedly paid a high personal cost in doing so since it meant they would be cut off and ostracized from their families and friends. Others, like the Jews of Medina, were asked to make a shift of a different sort. They were called to leave behind their previous understanding of monotheism and embrace a new one being preached by a man whose message was both similar to and different from the one to which they had grown accustomed.

Those who accepted the invitation could not leave their backgrounds behind. They brought their previous experiences and ideas with them when they entered the Islamic community. Former Jews and former polytheists now prayed side-by-side, and their prior religious lives helped to shape how they understood their present situation as fellow Muslims. In other words, many different people from a variety of backgrounds and perspectives had a hand in creating and shaping the community that gathered around

Muhammad. This was how Islam started, and it was a sign of things to come.

EXPANSION AND GROWTH

Soon after Muhammad's death in 632, Islam began to spread throughout the world, and this process has continued into the present day. Like Christianity, Islam is expansionist by nature as it seeks to attract and invite new members into its ranks. Consequently, people from many different backgrounds and cultures have joined the faith since its inception. This has enriched the community enormously by adding to its complexity and diversity.

We can get a sense of this by considering where Muslims are found today. Many people are surprised to learn that the Arabic-speaking world contains less than one-fifth of the entire Muslim population. Put another way, approximately four out of every five Muslims alive today reside in a place whose language, history, and culture have nothing in common with that of the Prophet Muhammad. According to a study conducted by the Pew Research Center, the following ten countries had the largest number of Muslims in 2010:

1. Indonesia (209 million)
2. India (176 million)
3. Pakistan (167 million)
4. Bangladesh (134 million)
5. Nigeria (77 million)
6. Egypt (76 million)
7. Iran (73 million)

8. Turkey (71 million)
9. Algeria (34 million)
10. Morocco (31 million)

Almost one-half of the Muslims in the world reside in the first five nations on that list, and not a single one of those countries is in the Arab world. Three of the next five are Arab countries, with Algeria and Morocco barely making the list. According to the same Pew Research Center study, by the year 2050, those two countries will fall out of the top ten, and Iraq will join Egypt as the lone representatives from the Arab world. In addition, both India and Pakistan will jump ahead of Indonesia to claim the top two spots by the middle of the twenty-first century.

This distribution shows what a mistake it is to identify Islam solely with the Middle East, as many non-Muslims do. It began in that region and its holy book was originally written in Arabic, but the vast majority of those who follow the faith are from other parts of the world and they will never set foot in the Middle East. Just as in the early days of the Muslim community, all those people of diverse backgrounds and experiences have had a profound impact on what Islam has become and what it will be in the future.

In the minds of many Muslims, the Arab world has a special status as the birthplace of their religion, but their own cultures play an equally important role in shaping their Islamic identity. We can see this in certain practices that are permitted in some parts of the Muslim world but forbidden in others. For example, in India it is not uncommon to find holy cards and other objects that depict Muhammad. Such things would never be found in the Middle East, where representations of the Prophet are considered to be in violation of Islam's prohibition against images. The social context and cultural norms of India allow these pictures to be tolerated in a way that is not possible in a place like Saudi Arabia. Numerous other examples of this phenomenon could be cited.

Such differences are important, but their role and effect should not be exaggerated. There is a very strong sense of community within Islam that can be traced back to its earliest days. The unity of all believers was a central theme of Muhammad's message as he sought to break down the walls that divided his contemporaries along tribal and religious lines. "You are the best community ever brought forth among people. You command what it good, you forbid what is evil, and you worship Allah" (Qur'an 3:110). The Arabic term for this notion of community is *ummah*, a word that appears with great frequency in the early Islamic sources and continues to shape Muslim identity into the present day. As already noted, realizing this communal ideal was not always easy for Muhammad. It became even more difficult as Islam spread and moved beyond the confines of the Arabian Peninsula and encountered other lands.

Muhammad's death led to the creation of an institution known as the caliphate. The term comes from the Arabic word *khalīfah* (caliph, in English) that refers to someone who rules or exercises authority in place of another. The first four men who held this office, who are usually referred to as the "rightly-guided caliphs," knew Muhammad personally and were chosen to lead because of their association with him. This period (632–661) was one of impressive growth for Islam. Less than thirty years after the Prophet's death, Islam established a strong presence in Egypt to the west, replaced the Sassanian Empire of Persia to the east, and gained a significant foothold in the Christian Byzantine Empire to the north. The *ummah* now extended from Egypt, across the Arabian peninsula, and into modern-day Syria and Iran.

The death of Ali, the last of the four rightly-guided caliphs, in 661 brought some major changes. Because it was situated on the periphery of a rapidly expanding empire, Medina was no longer a viable capital. It was replaced by Damascus, a former Byzantine center, and the caliphate entered what is known as the Umayyad Period (661–750). During this time, growth continued unabated as Islam now reached into North Africa, Spain, Portugal, France, and India.

Dissatisfaction with the Umayyad leadership led to yet another shift as the capital was moved to Baghdad, a new city, and the Abbasid Period (750–1258) of the caliphate commenced. This was the golden age of Islam when its influence and prominence were unrivaled. Muslims made significant contributions and advancements in the fields of science, art, literature, architecture, and philosophy whose marks are still evident today. Great cities like Cairo in Egypt, Cordoba in Spain, and Palermo in Italy were founded and became centers of learning and culture.

It all came crashing down in 1258 when the Mongols invaded Baghdad, ransacked the city, and brought the caliphate to an official end. In fact, the caliphate had ceased to function as an overarching, recognized authority quite some time before that. The Islamic empire had become so vast and intricate that it was impossible for one individual to control and govern the entire thing. Independent provinces and states had begun to emerge, and the unification of the *ummah* under one supreme authority was nothing more than an illusion by the eleventh century.

But the breakup of centralized authority did not mean the downfall of Islam. The Mongols themselves converted to the faith in order to legitimate their claim to authority. In later times, Islam continued to exert powerful influence throughout the world as seen in the establishment of the Safavid (Persian, 1502–1736), Mughal (Indian, 1526–1707), and Ottoman (Turkish, 1301–1922) empires, with the latter continuing to exist until the early-twentieth century.

This brief survey of the rise and spread of Islam raises a number of important issues. The first concerns the reasons behind the quick expansion. Why was Islam so readily accepted by those with whom it came in contact? For the Muslim, this success is clear evidence of God's favor—Allah rewarded the community for faithfully following the divine will. Beyond this, there are other factors that can help explain the events in non-theological, more objective terms.

Many non-Muslims have a mistaken understanding of how Islam spread. Contrary to a common perception, it was not accomplished by primarily violent means that forced people to convert. Such an approach would go against the Muslim view of religious faith that is reflected in an important Qur'an passage that says, "There is no compulsion in religion" (2:256). Local populations were given a number of options when Islamic forces entered their territory. They were first invited to join the faith and become Muslims. If they chose to do so, they were accepted as full members of the *ummah* and were granted all rights that went along with that status. A second option available to Jews and Christians was that they could keep their faith as long as they paid a special tax called the *jizyah*. This placed them in the category of the *dhimmi*, or protected minorities, and gave them freedom of religion to worship as they wished. Only in the event that neither of these two options was taken did military confrontation and violence ensue.

But this final scenario was quite rare. Most non-Muslims either converted to Islam or chose to enter the ranks of the *dhimmi*. This latter choice was a very appealing one for Jews and Christians since the Muslim authorities tended to adopt a hands-off approach in how they governed their people that was in marked contrast to other powers. The Byzantine Empire, in particular, often made life very difficult for those who came under its rule. Ironically, then, many non-Muslims fared better under Islam than they did under the Christian Byzantines.

A second issue relates to the focus of this chapter—the spread of Islam contributed to the complexity and diversity of the community. As it came in contact with people in various parts of Asia, Africa, and Europe, these experiences left their mark on the *ummah* in many ways. Converts to the faith brought with them rich backgrounds and talents that were now put in the service of Islam. In Spain and many other places, Jews and Christians lived and worked side-by-side with Muslims and all three communities benefited from the experience. Within a century of its founding, Islam had developed far beyond its humble origin in western Arabia and was now a major presence throughout the known world. As this process unfolded, the Muslim community was shaped and transformed by its exposure to new places and ideas, and it manifested itself differently in new contexts.

Not all contact between Islam and the rest of the world was positive in nature. At times, Muslims and non-Muslims found themselves at odds and expressed their disagreements in antagonistic, sometimes hostile, ways. The primary example of this is the series of military encounters known as the Crusades. From the late-eleventh until the late-thirteenth centuries Western Christendom engaged in a number of forays into Muslim territory, principally the Holy Land, with the intent of liberating and reclaiming Christian land that had fallen into the hands of "infidels." This chapter in Muslim-Christian relations resulted in feelings of hatred and mistrust that have sometimes continued into the present day. An example of this was seen when, in the immediate aftermath of the terrorist attacks that took place in the United States on September 11, 2001, President George W. Bush alluded to the imminent US response by saying, "This crusade, this war on terrorism, is going to take a while." That comment was sharply criticized by many people as being an insensitive remark that fed into and confirmed suspicions held by some

Muslims (and non-Muslims) regarding Western attitudes toward Islam.

The experience of colonization by European powers has had a similar effect in most Muslim countries. A number of Western European states, especially England, France, and the Netherlands, occupied and controlled areas with large Muslim populations for an extended period of time beginning in the eighteenth century. It was only in the mid-twentieth century that many of these areas were able to officially free themselves from the shackles of foreign domination. On occasion, modern interventions in Muslim countries by Western powers have been interpreted as forms of neocolonialism that allow them to exploit the resources of the Islamic world for their own benefit. For example, after the US-led invasion of Iraq in 2003, coalition forces allowed looters to ransack the National Museum in Baghdad and steal priceless objects from the ancient world while they stood guard outside the Ministry of Oil to make sure it was protected. Many equated that response with similar ones during the period of colonialism, and interpreted it as an indication of the true nature of American interests in the Middle East. Such experiences dredge up painful memories throughout the Islamic world, and Muslims have tried to address the issue of foreign influence in a number of different ways. This is a topic that will be treated shortly. First, a few other examples of diversity within the *ummah* will be considered.

THE SUNNI/SHI'I DIFFERENCE

Many non-Muslims are aware of the distinction between Sunni and Shi'i (often written Shi'ite) Islam. Among them are people in the United States who recall the tensions between their country and Iran that began with the Iranian revolution of 1979 and have only recently begun to ease. Until his death in 1989, many Americans identified the Shi'i religious leader Ayatollah Khomeini as the quintessential Muslim. In fact, however, the branch of Islam to which he belonged was not that of the majority of Muslims.

Estimates on the precise number of Shi'i Muslims vary, but it would be accurate to say that they constitute no more than 15 percent of the worldwide Muslim population. The countries with the most significant presence are Iran, Iraq, and Lebanon, but pockets of Shi'i are found throughout the Muslim world.

The group traces its roots to the earliest days of Islam, and it emerged primarily in response to the issue of who should have taken Muhammad's place after his death. From the very beginning there was a faction who felt that Ali, the Prophet's cousin and son-in-law, was uniquely qualified to serve as successor. Ali was passed over for this honor three successive times until he finally took control of the *ummah* as the fourth of the rightly-guided caliphs. Those who supported him felt slighted by this because they maintained that Muhammad himself chose Ali as his successor, and they cited prophetic traditions, or *hadīth*, to back up this claim. These supporters, or partisans, helped to give a name to the movement—the

Arabic word *shi'a* refers to a party of people who back a particular cause.

When Ali was assassinated in 661, his followers believed the caliphate should stay in his family. By virtue of his marriage to Muhammad's daughter Fatima, this would have also kept authority within the Prophet's line. Others were resistant to this idea, and they ultimately took control of the caliphate and established the Umayyad dynasty mentioned earlier. This is the Sunni branch of Islam, the majority group within the community until today.

A significant event occurred in the year 680, when Ali's son Husayn and his supporters were killed by Umayyad forces in the city of Karbala in modern-day Iraq. He was on his way to Damascus to reclaim the caliphate he believed was rightfully his when his group was attacked and brutally defeated. Husayn's martyrdom left an indelible mark on Shi'i Islam and was such a paradigmatic event that it is recalled and reenacted by the community each year on the tenth day of the month of Muharram in a ceremony that is full of lamentations and mourning rituals.

Throughout history, Shi'i Muslims have tended to view themselves as a marginalized, oppressed group that has been treated unfairly and denied what they believe to be rightfully theirs. Consequently, this branch of Islam preaches the importance of perseverance during suffering and tolerance under unjust circumstances. A term commonly associated with Shi'i Islam that is sometimes misunderstood by non-Muslims is that of *taqiyyah*, often translated as "necessary dissimulation." Based on certain verses in the Qur'an, this concept permits a person to deny what they truly believe, or to engage in activities that go against those beliefs, if failing to do so would lead to persecution or result in personal danger or death. This has led some non-Muslims at times to claim that Islam teaches its followers to lie and deceive others, but that is to misunderstand the true nature of *taqiyyah*. Its purpose is to protect Muslims, like oppressed Shi'i, who find themselves in precarious situations and must resort to the practice in order to survive.

From its inception, the Shi'i community was led by a series of rulers known as Imams who all traced their lineage back to Ali. Because they posed a potential threat to the authority of the Sunni caliphs, the Imams were often mistreated and suppressed by the majority. It is a central element of Shi'i belief that at a certain point in time the Imam was forced to go into hiding in order to protect himself and to ensure the continuation of the line. Most Shi'i believe it was the twelfth Imam who went into hiding in the tenth century. Others maintain that it was the seventh Imam. On this matter we see an example of the diversity that exists within the Shi'i branch of Islam. All agree, however, that the hidden Imam will return at the end of the world to vindicate his followers and usher in a final age of peace and prosperity for Muslims. The expectation that the hidden Imam will return one day is one of Shi'i Islam's characteristic features.

Sunni Muslims do not share this belief, but they do consider Shi'i to be fellow Muslims. Certain other differences exist between the two groups but they are relatively minor. For example, a set of *hadīth* that are traced back to the first

Imam Ali is an important resource within Shi'i Islam that does not play that same role for Sunni Muslims. All Muslims, regardless of their affiliation, engage in the same basic practices and hold the same beliefs. The primary difference between Sunni and Shi'i Muslims concerns the issue of leadership and authority. The differences that exist between Catholics and Protestants in the Christian tradition can serve as a helpful analogy in this regard.

SUFISM

We can see another example of diversity within Islam in Sufism, the mystical dimension of the faith. The term *Sufi* comes from the Arabic word for wool, and it probably refers to a distinctive style of dress adopted by Islamic mystics. As is the case with mystics in other religions, Sufis maintain that it is possible to engage in practices and activities that can allow one to experience God in such a personal way that the perceived division between the believer and the deity disappears and is recognized as merely an illusion.

This is a movement that goes back to the first decades of Islam, and many Sufis claim their approach is based on the earliest Islamic sources. Some have cited *hadīth* like Muhammad's statement, "My poverty is my pride," to find prophetic support for the ascetic lifestyle adopted by many Sufis. Others turn to the Qur'an and interpret passages like 50:16 ("We [Allah] are closer to a person than his jugular vein.") as justification for the idea that it is possible for a Muslim to have experiential knowledge of Allah.

The rise of the caliphate and its association with wealth and power undoubtedly had much to do with the development of Sufism. As the empire spread, those in positions of authority became more interested in political issues and the accumulation of possessions and, in the view of some Muslims, their commitment to Islam was diminished. Sufism arose as a corrective to this and a call for people to return to the essentials of the faith. Various Sufi orders developed over the centuries, each usually centered around the teachings of a founding figure, and many of them continue to attract members throughout the world into the present day.

But not all Muslims have agreed that what Sufism teaches is actually in line with orthodox Islamic belief. The idea that one can personally experience Allah has struck some as a dangerous idea because it runs the risk of erasing the distinction between God and believer. The absolute transcendence of Allah—and therefore a person's inability to ever truly know the divine nature—is a core belief of Islam. Throughout history, some have said that Sufism appears to violate this principle. Its goal is *fanā'*, or extinction of the self, which can be achieved through *dhikr*, or remembrance of Allah, a concept found frequently in the Qur'an (2:152; 7:205; 33:41). Sufi groups have developed many different methods, including chant, repeated phrases or body movements, and dance to assist their members in remembering Allah. One of the most well-known groups is the Whirling Dervishes, whose primary means of union with Allah is through their carefully choreographed dance sessions set to music that can go on for hours at a time. Non-Sufis have sometimes opposed such practices as innovations that have no place in Islam.

Some of these criticisms have been justified because abuses have crept into Sufism from time to time. A particularly controversial element is the practice of venerating the founders of Sufi orders and other holy men and women. Sometimes their burial places become shrines that attract Muslim pilgrims from around the world who come to celebrate the holy person's birthday. An example is the grave of Jelal al-Din Rumi (d. 1273), the founder of the Mevlevi order of the Whirling Dervishes. Thousands of people, both Muslim and non-Muslim, travel to the city of Konya in Turkey every year to visit the shrine that contains his remains and to seek his blessing. Such popular practices centered around individual Sufi figures are sometimes decried by critics as tantamount to saint worship and in opposition to Islam.

These criticisms notwithstanding, Sufism has contributed a great deal to Islam, and it remains a popular expression of the faith in many parts of the world. It has introduced new ways of thinking and talking about God that go far beyond the more abstract and theoretical approaches that have tended to dominate Islamic theological discourse. Rabi'a al-'Adawiya (d. 801) shocked some of her contemporaries when she spoke of Allah as her lover and described her relationship with God in erotic terms. But this was an image that enriched Islam and gave Muslims a new way of imagining God. The same might be said for Rumi, mentioned above, whose writings are so popular outside the Muslim world that translations of them make him one of the best-selling poets in the English language more than seven centuries after his death. Islam is forever indebted to him for the insights on the divine-human relationship that his writings, like this brief poem, have offered:

> A craftsman pulled a reed from the
>   reed bed,
> cut holes in it, and called it a human
>   being.
> Since then, it's been wailing a tender
>   agony
> of parting, never mentioning the skill
>   that gave it life as a flute.

DIVERSITY AND NON-MUSLIMS

The focus of this chapter has been the complex and diverse nature of Islam. From the very beginning, Muslims have lived out their faith in a variety of ways. The *ummah* is a single entity, but there are different ways of expressing membership in that one community. Non-Muslims must always keep this fact in mind when thinking about the actions or statements of individual Muslims. A final aspect of the diversity within Islam deserves special mention in this regard.

An important area of debate among Muslims, one that dates back to the earliest days of the religion, concerns how they should relate to non-Muslims. In modern times, Islam's relationship with the western world has often been the focus of attention. While many Muslims are open and receptive to ideas and influence from the West, others have been more cautious in their response, at times even to the point of hostility.

Some of this hesitancy is due to the negative experiences many Muslim countries had to endure during the years they were colonized by European powers. It is also partly due to the conservative nature of Islam. This is not meant in a pejorative sense—it simply refers to the tendency in Islam to look back to the time of the Prophet Muhammad and the early Islamic community as a model to follow. Lifestyles and ways of thinking that are perceived as not in agreement with that prophetic ideal, or are considered to be a threat to it, are often viewed cautiously.

There is a wide range of opinions within Islam regarding how to relate to the western world. Most Muslims prefer to interact with non-Muslims in a spirit of tolerance and dialogue, and some even maintain that Islam needs to adapt itself to become more like the West. A very small number of Muslims believe that violence and confrontation are the only proper responses in the face of what they consider to be western aggression. In recent times, this latter perspective has been adopted by people like Osama bin Laden and organizations like ISIS.

It is important for non-Muslims to avoid making generalizations about Islam when members of this last group engage in violence or terrorist activities under the guise of Islam. The easiest way to prevent this from happening is to listen to what the rest of the Islamic world is saying. Virtually all Muslims denounce such actions as not representing their faith, and those who are non-Muslims should view those actions in the same way.

QUESTIONS FOR DISCUSSION

1. What are some of your stereotypes of Islam? Where do they come from?

2. What are some stereotypes others might have of your religion? What is your reaction to them?

3. Identify some of the advantages and disadvantages of diversity within a religious community. Do you think diversity is a primarily negative or positive quality in a religion?

4. What can you do that will allow you to better understand and appreciate the complexity found in Islam?

5. What are some of the most significant barriers that can prevent someone from acknowledging the diversity that exists within Islam?

2

Islam Is a Religion of Orthopraxy

Act! God will see your actions, and so will His messenger and those who believe. For you will be returned to the One who knows the unseen and the seen, and He will inform you of what you were doing.
—Qur'an 9:105

Being a member of a religious community entails both holding certain beliefs and expressing those beliefs in action. In other words, the content of one's faith and the way that faith is lived out are essential elements of any religion. But the relationship between belief and action is not the same in all religions since the expressed proportion of the two dimensions varies among them. This has sometimes caused scholars and theologians to make a distinction between religions of orthodoxy and religions of orthopraxy.

A religion of orthodoxy (literally, "proper belief") is one in which the content of a person's faith is the critical component in determining whether or not he or she is truly a member of the community. In such a religion, having proper belief is what ultimately indicates the individual's status in relationship to its other followers. Christianity is often cited as an example of a religion of orthodoxy since adherence to particular beliefs, such as Jesus' divinity and the trinity, is what most clearly identifies one as a Christian.

Islam, on the other hand, is a prime example of a religion of orthopraxy (literally, "proper practice"). In a religion of this type, proper belief is not the sole or primary indicator of faith—proper action is just as important as what one believes, and it is often considered the true mark of one's membership in the community. This is not to say that correct action is inconsequential in a religion of orthodoxy or that proper belief does not matter in a system that stresses orthopraxy. Rather, it is a question of where the emphasis is placed in a given religion. The two should be thought of as existing on a continuum, with orthopraxy at one end and orthodoxy at the other—every religion gravitates toward one pole of the spectrum or the other, but it always contains elements of both. In religions of orthopraxy like Islam, actions express and articulate faith, and this is an important facet of the faith that non-Muslims should keep in mind. The Qur'an passage that opens this chapter communicates this idea very well. It states that faith-based actions are the means by which others recognize one's commitment to Islam, and that those actions will also be examined by Allah to judge the quality of a person's life. A Muslim's fate after death is determined by how well he or she puts belief into action.

THE *ḤADĪTH*

Before considering some of the ways Muslims express their
faith through their actions, it is important to first discuss the
importance of the *ḥadīth*, a term introduced in the previous
chapter. When looking for guidance on how to be a good
Muslim, the early community naturally turned to the Prophet
Muhammad as a model. The Qur'an offers much instruction
on how people should conduct themselves, but it does not
address every situation and circumstance a person might have
to confront. It was therefore natural that early Muslims would
often ask the question "What would Muhammad do?" when
they sought assistance on matters not treated in their sacred
text. During his life they could ask him directly, but after
his death his family members and others who knew him
personally shared their recollections of what Muhammad said
or did while he was among them. Over time, these stories
began to accumulate and circulate among members of the
ummah. This material was extremely important since it set an
example of what proper Muslim behavior should be.

Each of these prophetic traditions is called a *ḥadīth*, an
Arabic term meaning "report" or "account," and is composed
of two parts. The first is a list of names that identifies the chain
of transmission of the report in the form "*A* heard from *B*,
who heard from *C* . . ." and eventually ends with Muhammad
himself. The second part is the body of the tradition that
recounts something the Prophet said or did. The following
example contains a saying from Muhammad regarding the
consumption of alcohol:

'Abd Allah ibn Yusuf told us that Malik informed him on the authority of Nafi' from Ibn 'Umar, may God be pleased with him, that the Messenger of God, may the prayers and peace of God be with him, said, "Whoever drinks wine in this world and does not repent of it will find it forbidden in the hereafter."

Thousands of these prophetic traditions were in circulation in the centuries after Muhammad's death. By the ninth century CE, some individuals began the tedious process of traveling throughout the Islamic world to collect and study the *hadīth* material. A particularly crucial issue for them was that of reliability—which traditions went back to Muhammad himself, and which ones were fabrications? On this matter, the chain of transmitters offered some important clues. If a list was comprised of trustworthy individuals and it had no chronological gaps, it was more likely to be viewed as authentic. On the other hand, if someone in the list of transmitters was known to be of dubious moral character, or two consecutive transmitters could not have known each other, the *hadīth* would be called into question.

A science of *hadīth* criticism and study emerged in order to address these questions, and each tradition was placed in one of several categories: sound, acceptable, or weak, with those in the third category being rejected as not authentic. The role of the prophetic traditions in Islam has been a point of contention, particularly in recent times. A number of Muslim scholars view them cautiously, and some have rejected them outright because of their questionable reliability. For example, at times reservations about the traditions have been expressed because it would have been easy for someone to create a *ḥadīth* by simply attaching an acceptable chain of transmitters to something Muhammad had purportedly said, and then pass it off as legitimate. Despite these occasional misgivings, the *ḥadīth* material continues to play a very prominent role in the lives of most Muslims, for whom they function as a window into the Prophet's world and his understanding of Islam. Two of the most well-respected collections are those of al-Bukhari (d. 870) and Muslim (d. 874). Each contains several thousand *ḥadīth* and covers a wide range of topics. A popular Arabic-English printed edition of al-Bukhari's collection is nine volumes in length, and treats matters as diverse as the proper form of communal prayer and the most intimate matters of personal hygiene. Many searchable websites containing the *ḥadīth* are now readily available, and one of the most useful can be found at the following link: http://sunnah.com/. The wide range of subjects discussed in the *ḥadīth* collections gives a clear sense of the important role Muhammad plays as a model for Muslims. The customary way he spoke and acted (the Arabic word for this is *sunnah*, which means "path") is the example for all Muslims to follow.

THE FIVE PILLARS

Muslims live out their faith in a variety of ways, but five activities enjoy pride of place as the "pillars" of Islam. These five practices are required of all Muslims, and they are the most visible ways one expresses his or her identity as a member of the *ummah*. Each of these pillars goes back to the earliest days of Islam, and references to them are sometimes found in both the Qur'an and the *hadīth*.

1. PROFESSION OF FAITH

The first pillar is the profession of faith (*shahādah* in Arabic). Like many religions, Islam has a creed that articulates its essence and summarizes its core beliefs. The Muslim creed is quite brief and consists of two parts: "I testify that there is no God but Allah, and Muhammad is Allah's messenger." This statement succinctly encapsulates two ideas that are central to Islamic theology. The first part expresses a monotheism that negates the existence of all deities but the one God. The unity of Allah is the defining feature of the Muslim understanding of God, and anything that disrupts that unity is considered to be the most serious of sins. The term commonly used for this offense is *shirk* (literally, "association"), which describes the attempt to join or associate something from the created world with the uncreated nature of Allah in a way that violates the divine unity. Examples of this would be worshipping an idol that has been fashioned by human hands, or ascribing divinity to a living being. According to the Qur'an, *shirk* is the only sin that God will not forgive (4:48, 116).

The second part of the creed underscores the critical role Muhammad plays in Islam. He is identified as a messenger, a status that very few individuals have attained. In the Islamic understanding of revelation, throughout history Allah has sent prophets to particular peoples in order to remind them of the divine will. The Qur'an identifies approximately two dozen prophets by name, most of them figures who are also mentioned in the Bible. Several of these prophets, like Moses, David, Jesus, and Muhammad, are also given the title "messenger." It is unclear what the precise difference is between a prophet and a messenger in the Qur'an. Since the four messengers just mentioned came to their people with a written text, it has sometimes been suggested that this is the defining feature of a messenger. But this idea is incorrect since some individuals identified as messengers in the Qur'an, like Ishmael, were not given a book. Despite this uncertainty regarding what the office entails, it is clear that messengers like Muhammad have a special status within Islam. The relationship between Muhammad and the prior messengers will be discussed in the next chapter. For now, it is important to note that when the Muslim creed speaks of him as a messenger, it is giving him a title that has rarely been bestowed on an individual.

The profession of faith functions in a variety of ways in Islam. Like all creeds, it is often recited to express one's membership in the community and personal assent to the teachings of the faith. It is also sometimes spoken at key moments in one's life. Muslim parents whisper it into the ears of newborns in order to have them hear as early as possible what they hope will become the child's own statement of belief when he or she grows up. Those who recite the creed with their last breath are specially blessed for dying with it on their lips. For converts to Islam, recitation of the profession of faith with the intent of becoming a Muslim is the way one becomes a member of the *ummah*. It is also included as part of the Muslim public call to prayer, which begins, "God is great! God is great! God is great! God is great! I testify that there is no God but Allah and Muhammad is Allah's messenger." Similarly, the prayer call ends by reciting the first half of the *shahādah*—"There is no God but Allah!" Consequently, even non-Muslims who live in an area with a strong Muslim presence hear the Islamic profession of faith at least five times a day. These and other ways in which the profession of faith is recited by Muslims indicate that there is a performative dimension to its proclamation that makes it an action expressing one's belief and membership in the *ummah*.

2. PRAYER

The second pillar of faith is prayer (*ṣalāt*). All believers are expected to pray five times each day, and most non-Muslims have seen images of Muslims engaged in this ritual. In the typical scene, rows of people are neatly lined up and making body movements in unison with such precision that they appear to be choreographed. The picture usually leaves a lasting and visually pleasing impression on the mind.

Islamic prayers follow carefully prescribed rubrics. The prayer times are determined by the position of the sun in the sky, and they take place over the course of the day at dawn, noon, mid-afternoon, sunset, and evening. Muslims are summoned by the call to prayer, and they are encouraged to fulfill their obligation at the mosque, or *masjid* (literally, "place of prostration"). Most, however, prefer to pray elsewhere, and it is common in Islamic countries to see people engaged in prayer in their workplaces and in public spaces. The only time prayer in a mosque is required is at noon on Friday, when the entire congregation joins together and, in addition to the usual ritual, hears a sermon preached by the *imām*, or leader of the local community. (This title is the same one that is used for the leader of the Shi'i community, but here it refers to an entirely different office.) Attendance at Friday noon prayer is required only of men. Women may attend services if they wish, but when they do so they typically pray in an area separate from the men.

Attached to many mosques is a minaret (*manārah* in Arabic), a tower from which the call to prayer is recited. In earlier times, this was the place from which the man known as the *muezzin* would summon Muslims to the mosque at prayer times by climbing to the top and proclaiming the call in a loud voice. In most places today, this is now done by a recording that is broadcast over a loudspeaker. The call to prayer, or *adhān*, is the following:

> Allah is great! (repeated four times)
> I testify that there is no God but Allah (repeated twice)
> I testify that Muhammad is Allah's messenger (repeated twice)
> Come to prayer! (repeated twice)
> Come to prosperity! (repeated twice)
> Allah is great! (repeated twice)
> There is no God but Allah!

The call is the same for all five prayer times except the first one at dawn, when there is a gentle reminder to get out of bed with the addition of the line "Prayer is better than sleep."

Whether praying alone or in a group, one must first be ritually clean. This entails removing one's shoes and going through a purification process in which the hands, mouth, face, and feet are washed. The requirement of ritual cleansing explains why fountains with flowing water are typically an essential element of the architecture of a mosque. Those praying outside a mosque commonly make use of a prayer mat. Muslims must always face the holy city of Mecca when praying. Getting one's bearing in a mosque is facilitated by the orientation of the building and the presence of a niche called the *miḥrāb* that indicates the *qiblah*, or direction toward Mecca.

As the Arabic word for mosque suggests, Islamic prayer includes prostration and other bodily movements. The basic unit of prayer is called a *rakʿah*, a word that comes from the Arabic verb "to bow down." Each *rakʿah* begins with the phrase, "God is great," and includes prostrations, bows, prescribed prayers, and brief Qur'an passages. Each *rakʿah* takes no more than a few minutes to complete and, depending on the time of day, between two and four of them must be done to fulfill the obligation to pray.

Many Muslims speak quite movingly of this aspect of their faith lives. The experience of praying together in a large congregation where everyone is engaged in the same movements can engender a profound sense of unity.

Similarly, many draw attention to the fact that the worldwide presence of Islam means that as the sun makes its way across the sky Muslims are praying twenty-four hours a day.

The Qur'an repeatedly mentions the injunction to pray. "Watch over prayers, especially the middle prayer. Stand obediently before Allah" (2:238). Despite the reference to the "middle prayer" in this verse, Islam's sacred text does not specify when or how many times a day a person should pray. But the *hadīth* material is quite clear on this point and traces the five daily prayer times back to the Prophet himself. Prayer is a topic that is extensively discussed in the *hadīth*, and the collection of prophetic sayings has approximately 1,400 separate traditions related to it. As the following examples indicate, even seemingly insignificant details are addressed in the prophetic traditions that treat prayer:

> Abu Huraira reported that a person addressed the Messenger of Allah (may peace be upon him) and said to him, "Can any one of us say prayer in one garment?" He said, "Do all of you possess two garments?"
>
> Jabir b. Samura reported that the Messenger of Allah (may peace be upon him) said, "The people who lift their eyes towards the sky in prayer should avoid it or they will lose their eyesight."

3. ALMSGIVING

Giving alms (*zakāt*) is the third pillar. The text of Qur'an 2:277 describes the benefits that await those who freely give of their resources to help others. "Truly, those who believe, and do good deeds, and observe prayer, and give alms have their reward from their Lord. Fear will not come upon them nor will they grieve." This passage lists a number of things required of Muslims: belief, good deeds, prayer, and almsgiving. It is interesting that this list, or portions of it, appears with great frequency in the Qur'an. In particular, the pairing of prayer with almsgiving is found consistently throughout Islam's sacred text. The term *zakāt*, referring to the requirement to give alms, occurs thirty times in the Qur'an. In all but three of those cases it is preceded, as here, by a reference to the practice of prayer.

This relationship is a clear indication of the connection between faith and action in Islam. It is not enough to say one's prayers and believe in Allah—Muslims must also meet their obligations to their fellow believers. In other words, there is a social dimension to the religion that says faith in God and commitment to others must go hand-in-hand. This is why giving alms is considered to be an essential element of Islam that is required of all adults who are able to fulfill the obligation.

The Qur'an never specifies what percentage of one's wealth should be given as *zakāt*. The general consensus among Muslims is that two and one-half percent of one's accumulated assets (not just income) should be given for this purpose. It is important to note that this is not seen as an act of charity since it is not a voluntary offering. Rather, it is more like a debt that is owed to the community by virtue of one's membership in the *ummah*.

In the early days of Islam it was often the political

authorities who saw to it that the *zakāt* was paid and then distributed appropriately. Now it is primarily an individual responsibility or duty, although some countries have maintained their right to enforce this requirement. According to the Qur'an (9:60), the money that is collected is to be used to assist the poor and needy and those who work with them, in addition to helping those who are in debt or are wayfarers. The verse also says it is to be used in the "cause of Allah," a phrase that is usually interpreted to mean any activity that assists in the spread of Islam, including education or the building and maintenance of mosques. Despite the relatively anonymous nature of almsgiving in most places, this is a practice that Muslims take very seriously. According to the results of a Pew Research Center study of Muslims throughout the world published in 2012, in only three of the thirty-nine countries surveyed did less than 50 percent of the respondents say they gave alms each year, while in twenty-eight of the countries the rate was 70 percent or higher. (The full results of that study can be found here: http://www.pewforum.org/2012/08/09/the-worlds-muslims -unity-and-diversity-executive-summary/.)

Many *ḥadīth* describe the Prophet Muhammad's words and actions regarding the practice of giving alms. The following example, which comes through his wife Aisha, explains the benefit of the simplest act of kindness:

Aisha reported Allah's Messenger (may peace be upon him) as saying, "When a woman gives in charity some of the food in her house without causing any damage, there is reward for her for whatever she has given, and a reward for her husband for what he earned. The same applies to the trustee. In no respect does the one diminish the reward of the other."

4. FASTING

The fourth pillar of Islam is the annual fast (*ṣawm*). Throughout Ramadan, the ninth month of the year, all Muslims should engage in a total fast each day from dawn until dusk. This is a requirement for all who have reached maturity and can physically endure the experience. No food or drink is to be taken during daylight hours, smoking is prohibited, and people are to refrain from all sexual activity. Certain situations and conditions can free one from the obligation to fast at the prescribed times. For example, pregnant or nursing women, the sick, and those traveling great distances are not required to fast if doing so would put them at risk, but they should complete the fast as soon as they are able to do so. Similarly, the elderly and those with a sickness for which there is no hope of recovery are not expected to fast.

Muslim tradition associates the Ramadan fast with the beginning of the revelations received by Muhammad. According to Islamic sources, on the twenty-seventh night of the month, called the "Night of Power," the Qur'an was first revealed to him. Each year that day is one of special joy throughout the Islamic world as the community celebrates the reception of its sacred text.

Islam makes use of a lunar calendar that is approximately eleven days shorter than the solar calendar commonly used in the West. Consequently, the months are not fixed in a particular season or time of year—it takes each month about thirty-three years to pass through the cycle of solar seasons. Depending on where one is living, this means Ramadan often falls in a time of year that can be unbearably hot and uncomfortable. This is especially true for those living in warm climates who work outdoors and must go without water or other sustenance for the entire day. In recent times, Muslim migration to parts of the world in which Islam had little or no prior presence has sometimes led to challenging conditions during the Ramadan fast. This is the case in some areas of the Scandinavian countries, like Iceland and northern Norway and Sweden, where the sun dips below the horizon for just a brief period of time during the summer, if at all. When Ramadan falls during that time of year in those places, special accommodations have to be made for those fasting.

In many places in the Islamic world a siren, cannon, or some other loud sound signals the sun's setting each day during the month of Ramadan. This marks the beginning of *ifṭār*, the breaking of the fast, during which time families gather together for prayers and a meal. This is a joyous occasion that often includes a visit to the homes of relatives and friends or a trip to a local park or festival. One of the two most important feasts of the Muslim year occurs at the end of Ramadan when the fasting is completed and the tenth month begins. This celebration, known as *ʿīd al-fiṭr* ("Feast of Fast-Breaking"), lasts for several days during which people exchange gifts, share meals, and join in communal prayer. It is a national holiday in some Islamic countries. According to the Pew Research Center survey mentioned above, the Ramadan fast is a requirement that Muslims take very seriously. The only part of the Muslim-majority world in which at least two-thirds of the Muslim population does not fast is Central Asia, where just over one-half do so. In Southern and Eastern Europe about two-thirds of Muslims perform the annual fast, while in Africa and other parts of Asia the proportion rises to between 94 and 99 percent of all Muslims.

This pillar is well documented in the Qur'an and the *hadīth*. The basic requirements of the Ramadan fast are mentioned in Qur'an 2:185. "The month of Ramadan is the time when the Qur'an was sent down as a guidance for people with clear proofs of guidance and discernment. Whoever sees the new moon of the month should fast during it. But whoever is sick or on a journey may make up the fast on other days." As the following example illustrates, the *hadīth* collections address a variety of concerns and issues related to the annual fast:

> Abu Huraira reported that a person had intercourse with his wife during Ramadan while fasting. The man asked for a ruling on this from the Messenger of Allah. The holy Prophet said, "Can you find a slave and grant him freedom?" He said, "No." The Prophet asked, "Can you afford to observe the fast for two consecutive months?" He answered, "No." The Prophet said, "Then feed sixty poor men."

This prophetic tradition identifies another practice that is urged during the month of Ramadan. Muslims are expected to be particularly mindful of the poor during this time of year and to give generously to those in need. Other *ḥadīth* remind believers that those who donate money and food to the poor during Ramadan will be rewarded with extra blessings.

5. PILGRIMAGE

Pilgrimage (*ḥajj*) is the fifth pillar of Islam. All Muslim men who can afford it and are physically able to make the trip should, at some point in their lives, journey to Mecca and perform the rituals associated with the pilgrimage. Women are also encouraged to participate, but they must be accompanied by a male relative if they go. In several places, the Qur'an makes reference to the pilgrimage:

> The months of pilgrimage are known. If someone decides to undertake the pilgrimage in these months let there be no inappropriate speech, immorality, or quarreling during it. Allah knows the good that you do. Take provisions for the journey—obedience is the best of provisions. Obey Me, O people of understanding. (2:197)

The pilgrimage to Mecca is to be undertaken during the "month of the pilgrimage," the twelfth month of the year known as *Dhu al-Ḥijjah* in Arabic. This Qur'an passage's references to avoiding improper speech or actions underscore the importance of ritual purity during the pilgrimage. This is outwardly expressed by the clothing one wears while a pilgrim. All participants dress alike in white garments that are meant to express their state of purification while calling attention to their unity as fellow believers. Many modern-day Muslims speak of the overpowering sense of community they experience when they participate in the pilgrimage with millions of others who are dressed in identical fashion while performing the same rituals. In his autobiography, the prominent African American Muslim Malcolm X (d. 1965) described his pilgrimage to Mecca as the catalyst that caused him to break with the Nation of Islam and embrace Sunni Islam because it gave him a new appreciation for the diversity within the unity of the *ummah*. During the *ḥajj* the geographic, cultural, and socioeconomic distinctions among the participants disappear, and they are truly one community united in worship of Allah.

The pilgrimage entails completing a series of carefully prescribed rituals that take place over a week's time during the first half of the twelfth month. This is done in Mecca and the surrounding area, and the rituals include such activities as circling the *ka'bah* a set number of times, throwing pebbles at stone pillars that represent Satan, walking rapidly between two fixed sites within the confines of the Sacred Mosque at Mecca, and listening to a sermon as part of a full day spent on the Plain of Arafat outside the city. These and other rituals must be performed at particular times and in the proper manner. An informative video of what takes place during the pilgrimage is available at the following website: http://video.nationalgeographic.com/video/saudiarabia_ mecca?source=relatedvideo.

As noted in the previous chapter, worship at the *ka'bah* as a sacred site predates Muhammad and the emergence of Islam. While it served as a polytheistic shrine during the Prophet's lifetime, its origin was monotheistic according to

Islamic sources. The Qur'an and Muslim tradition identify it with Abraham, and they maintain that he and his son Ishmael were the ones who built the shrine as a place to worship the one true God.

> We [Allah] determined the location of the house for Abraham, and We said, "Do not associate anything with me. Cleanse My house for those who circumambulate it, those who stand in prayer, and those who prostrate themselves. And proclaim the pilgrimage to people so they will come on foot and on beast along distant roads." (22:26–27)

The association with Abraham helps to explain a number of rituals that are part of the pilgrimage. For example, as the pilgrims hurriedly walk back and forth between two locations, they are recalling and reenacting Hagar's frantic search for water for herself and her son Ishmael. Similarly, their tossing of pebbles is meant to be a reminder of Abraham's rejection of Satan's temptations. There is even a spot near the *ka'bah* called "the place of Abraham" that is considered to be the location where he and his son stood in prayer.

The pilgrimage comes to an end with a final ritual that also relates to Abraham's life. The pilgrims slaughter and eat sheep and other animals in a way that commemorates Abraham's near sacrifice of Isaac. As in the biblical tradition (Genesis 22), Islam teaches that God allowed an animal to be substituted for the son. The food that is not eaten by the pilgrims is distributed to the poor in keeping with the Islamic injunction to help those in need. As the pilgrims sacrifice their animals and share in meals, Muslims all over the world are doing the same thing as they celebrate the greatest feast of the year, '*īd al-'adhā* ("Feast of Sacrifice").

Many pilgrims decide to stay a bit longer after the pilgrimage to make a journey to Medina. Since this is the only time most of them will ever set foot in the Holy Land of Islam, they take the opportunity to visit other sites like Muhammad's mosque and burial place. Upon returning home, they now enjoy special status as a *hajj*, a title of honor given to those who have made the pilgrimage. Because of the high cost involved in traveling to Saudi Arabia and the expenses incurred while on the pilgrimage, relatively few Muslims are able to complete this pillar of the faith. Due to their relative proximity to Mecca, it should come as no surprise that the Pew Center survey found that the Middle East and North Africa had the largest percentage of Muslims (17%) who said they had completed the *hajj*. Although it does not fulfill the pilgrimage requirement, Muslims may also make an abbreviated visit to Mecca at any time during the year that is called an '*umrah* in which they engage in many of the same rituals that take place during the *hajj*.

As with the other pillars of the faith, there is a large body of *hadīth* material that discusses various aspects of the pilgrimage. The following example gives Muhammad's view on whether or not a child may make the pilgrimage:

> Ibn Abbas reported that Allah's Messenger (may peace be upon him) met some riders at al-Rauha and asked who they were. They replied that they were Muslims. They said, "Who are

you?" He said, "I am the Messenger of Allah." A woman lifted up a boy to him and asked, "Would this child be credited with having performed the pilgrimage?" He answered, "Yes, and you would be granted a reward."

POPULAR PRACTICES

This survey of the five pillars shows why Islam is commonly considered to be a religion of orthopraxy. Each of these practices requires putting faith into action and outwardly expressing what one believes. Profession of faith, prayer, almsgiving, fasting, and pilgrimage are not obligations that can be met in the recesses of one's heart or mind. They are public proclamations and visible manifestations of what is inside a person, and they literally put faith into action.

The pillars are five essential elements of Islam that are shared by all, but they are not the only ways Muslims show their faith. As with other religions, a host of other practices are also found, and the Islamic community has responded to them in various ways. Some of them are highly regarded and universally recognized as valid forms of worship within Islam. Others have been more controversial and have sometimes evoked a critical reaction that questions their legitimacy and appropriateness. A consideration of some of the more common and important of these popular practices will illustrate these different responses.

Prayer beads (called *subḥah*) are a common sight throughout the Muslim world. They resemble the rosaries found in the Catholic tradition, and they are usually comprised of a string of eleven or thirty-three beads. They are used to facilitate recitation of what is known as the "ninety-nine names of Allah." Several times in the Qur'an, reference is made to the names of Allah. "Allah—there is no God but He. To Him belong the most beautiful names" (20:8). An Islamic tradition developed from this and similar Qur'an passages that claims Allah possesses ninety-nine names, each describing some divine trait or quality. Many of these names come from the Qur'an, and the list includes such descriptors as "the Merciful," "the Highest," "the All-Seeing," and "the Sustainer." Many pious Muslims memorize the entire list of names or portions of it and use the *subḥah* to assist them in reciting them. The idea that God has ninety-nine names was somewhat controversial in the early days of Islam as people debated whether the names were at odds with the divine unity that is at the heart of Muslim theology. Some wondered if the names might somehow threaten that unity by encouraging worship of God under various guises like "the Mighty One" and "the Eternal One." Eventually, the names came to be viewed as nothing more than attributes or qualities of the one God that in no way undermine the deity's essential oneness. Reciting those names while thumbing a *subḥah* continues to be a common form of Muslim piety throughout the world.

The *'umrah*, or lesser pilgrimage, that was mentioned above is another popular practice that is prominent in Islam. Unlike the greater pilgrimage (*hajj*), the *'umrah* may be performed at any time during the year and takes only about one hour to complete. All of its rituals are done inside the Great Mosque in Mecca and are also part of the greater pilgrimage. The following *ḥadīth* traces this abbreviated form of the fifth pillar back to the time of the Prophet Muhammad. "Qatida said, 'I asked Anas how many pilgrimages had been accomplished by Allah's Messenger, and he replied that one *ḥajj* and four *'umrahs* were performed by him.'" The fact that the practice of making the *'umrah* was something that could be traced back to the life of the Prophet Muhammad himself did much to validate it in the eyes of later Muslims.

Other popular practices that are well established within Islam were referred to in the previous chapter. The *ta'zīyah* is an integral part of the faith lives of Shi'i Muslims. This reenactment of the martyrdom of Ali's son Husayn and his companions at Karbala in 680 is a kind of "passion play" that recalls this critical event and expresses important elements of Shi'i identity, especially their understanding of themselves as oppressed minorities who have been denied a status and authority that is rightfully theirs. Similarly, the chanting, dance, and many other rituals that are associated with Sufism are all accepted as valid forms of Muslim piety even for those who are not mystics themselves.

More problematic are certain activities that, in the minds of some, fall outside the range of acceptable Islamic behavior and even appear to violate core beliefs of the religion. A primary example of this is the veneration of holy men and women. Their birthdays are recalled, their tombs are visited, and miracles are sometimes ascribed to them. In certain places, these individuals have become so popular that feasts in their honor can last for several days. Similar gatherings are sometimes held throughout the Muslim world to recognize the death anniversary of important Sufi leaders. In South Asia this event is called an *'urs*, from an Arabic word that means "wedding," and sometimes thousands of people travel to the holy person's shrine or tomb for a time of remembrance and celebration. Some Muslims view such practices as a sinful innovation that does nothing but create a cult of saints in Islam, thereby running the risk of privileging these people in a way that makes them divine. One of the most outspoken critics against this aspect of the faith was Muhammad ibn 'Abd al-Wahhab (1703–92), who lived in Arabia and strongly condemned the beliefs and practices associated with Muslim saints. He gave his name to the Wahhabi movement that continues to exert influence in Saudi Arabia and elsewhere into the modern day.

Related to this phenomenon is the annual commemoration of Muhammad's birthday (called the *mawlid*) on the twelfth day of the third Islamic month. Despite its popularity, this celebration has also come under attack at times as an unnecessary novelty that is unsupported by Islamic theology and goes against Muhammad's own wishes. Despite those criticisms, it is a joyous occasion in many parts of the Islamic world, and it has spawned an impressive body of songs and poems that honor the Prophet. A popular style of Turkish poetry called a *mevlût* that commemorates Muhammad's birth is found in many different versions. It begins by telling the story of how the Prophet's mother Amina gave birth to him, followed by words of joy that all of creation uttered as he entered the world:

Welcome, O high prince, we welcome you!
Welcome, O mine of wisdom, we welcome you!
Welcome, O secret of the book, we welcome you!
Welcome, O medicine for pain, we welcome you!
Welcome, O sunlight and moonlight of God!
Welcome, O you not separated from God!
Welcome, O nightingale of the Garden of Beauty!
Welcome, O friend of the Lord of Power!
Welcome, O refuge of your community!
Welcome, O helper of the poor and destitute!
Welcome, O eternal soul, we welcome you!
Welcome, O cupbearer of the lovers, we welcome you!
Welcome, O darling of the Beloved!
Welcome, O much beloved of the Lord!
Welcome, O mercy for the worlds!
Welcome, O intercessor for the sinner!
Only for you were time and space created!

ORTHOPRAXY AND NON-MUSLIMS

In Islam, faith must be expressed in action. While the five pillars are the most common activities Muslims engage in as visible signs of what they believe, they are not the only ones. This is important background for understanding how and why some people engage in violence and then claim to be doing so in the name of Islam. It begins to explain why the perpetrators of the attacks on September 11, 2001 flew airplanes into buildings, why some individuals strap dynamite on themselves and try to kill as many people as possible, and why groups like ISIS behead innocent people and destroy treasured sites from the ancient world. Such deeds strike most people, including the vast majority of Muslims, as deranged and misguided. But for those who carry them out, they are religious acts that put their faith into practice.

This is related to the role of martyrdom in Islam, a concept that frequently makes headlines and is often misunderstood. In particular, the question of suicide has become an important one in recent times. The Islamic sources cannot be properly used to justify the actions of those who take their own lives while engaged in terrorist activities. In several places, the Qur'an states that those who die in the "way of Allah" will be rewarded. "Do not say of those who are killed in the way of Allah that they are dead. Rather, they are alive even if you do not know" (2:154). In one passage (47:6), their reward is specified as being admitted into gardens where they will enjoy eternal comfort.

In these and all other texts that discuss those who lose their lives in the "way of Allah" the passive voice is used—they are killed, they do not kill themselves. Dying for one's faith, particularly when defending what one believes, is highly regarded in Islam, just as it is in Judaism, Christianity, and other religions. The martyr or *shahīd* (literally, "witness") who makes the supreme sacrifice is therefore held up as a model for other Muslims.

But those who take their own lives in the name of their faith are not acting in the way of Allah. The Qur'an does not contain any clear references to the act of suicide, but two verses strongly suggest that killing oneself is morally wrong. The first is found in 2:195: "Spend in accord with God's way. Do not bring about your destruction by your own hands, but do good. Truly, God loves those who do good." The sense of the verse is broad enough to suggest that a ban on suicide can be included. The other verse contains a more direct admonition against killing. "Believers, do not vainly eat up each other's wealth, but engage in mutual trade fairly. Do not kill each other, for God is merciful to you" (4:29). The object of the verb "to kill" can be translated as either "each other" or "yourselves." According to the latter meaning, the verse can be interpreted as forbidding suicide. These two verses, as well as the Qur'an's general ethos to avoid murder and respect life, strongly suggest that the Islamic scripture forbids suicide. This is in agreement with several *ḥadīth* that have the Prophet Muhammad prohibiting the act.

Suicide bombers and others who kill themselves along with innocent people should not appeal to Islam to support their actions. They might attempt to do so, but all such attempts are bound to fail because they are based on twisted logic and faulty readings of the Islamic sources. This highlights the issue of interpretation, a theme to be discussed in more detail later. Any text or tradition can be interpreted in a variety of ways, but not all interpretations are proper or valid. Anyone who thinks the sources of Islam approve of suicide has misinterpreted the evidence.

The lesson for non-Muslims is similar to that found at the end of the first chapter. They should not draw conclusions about Islam as a whole from the actions of a few. They need to pay equal attention to the actions and responses of other Muslims. Many of them have put their faith into practice, sometimes at great personal risk, to speak out against violence and to assist those who have suffered as a result of terrorist attacks. This, more than anything, is Islam in action.

QUESTIONS FOR DISCUSSION

1. What similarities do you note between the practices of Islam and those found in other religions? How might those similarities be explained?
2. Do you find a religion of orthodoxy or a religion of orthopraxy more appealing?
3. Write down some examples of popular religious practices that you are familiar with. What kinds of issues do such activities raise for a religious community? What are some of the pros and cons of these practices?
4. Do religions of orthopraxy tend to be more violent than religions of orthodoxy?
5. What do you think should be the proper blend between orthodoxy and orthopraxy in a religion?

3

Muslims Respect Judaism and Christianity

O People of the Book, you have nothing until you observe the
Torah and the Gospel and what has been revealed to you from
your Lord.
—Qur'an 5:68

Jews and Christians sometimes believe Islam has a very low
opinion of their religions and that it encourages hostility
toward followers of the other monotheistic faiths. Nothing
could be further from the truth. This misperception can
prevent Jews and Christians from seeing Islam as it really is
and, in the process, miss the fact that it has much more in
common with their religions than they realize.

I was reminded of this once when I gave a lecture on
Islam at a church. After the session a man came up to me
and inquired, "Is it true that Muslims hate Jesus?" When
I finished my explanation of why it is not the case that
followers of Islam hate Jesus, several Muslim men who had

overheard the conversation stepped forward and offered their own perspectives. One of them made a statement that undoubtedly surprised the man who asked the question. He said, "It is impossible to be a Muslim and hate Jesus. In fact, a Muslim who does not love Jesus is not a true Muslim." The man was absolutely correct. It may shock some, but there is a deep and abiding respect for Judaism and Christianity at the core of Islam.

The relationships among members of the three monotheistic religions are very complex, and throughout history they have been influenced by many theological, historical, and political factors that continue to leave their mark. In other words, the context in which the followers of those religions find themselves plays a major role in shaping how they interact and express their differences. For example, the relationships among Jews, Christians, and Muslims living in Jerusalem are markedly different from those living in New York City. Those residing in the Middle East find themselves in a reality that is not shared by their American counterparts, and this difference in context is critical for determining how they relate to and understand each other.

It is the differences among Muslims, Christians, and Jews that tend to grab the headlines and dominate conversations. This has often been the case throughout history, but the situation has been exacerbated in our high-tech, digital society, which allows us to be transported instantly to another part of the world. The experience of "being there" can sometimes make the differences between "us" and "them" more pronounced and apparent while letting the similarities go unrecognized. This can be seen in the way ISIS and other terrorist organizations make use of Facebook, YouTube, and other forms of social media to publicize their activities and recruit new members. Unlike in earlier times, when such groups operated in the shadows and had very few ways of reaching a wide audience, their message is now immediately available to anyone with a computer, cell phone, or iPad anywhere in the world. Unfortunately, this technology is not used as often as it could be to showcase how close the religions of Muslims, Jews, and Christians are to one another.

In this chapter, some of these similarities and connections will be explored. It is important for the non-Muslim to be familiar with these points of contact because they help to explain the Islamic appreciation for Judaism and Christianity. In places, the connections and shared roots are so deep that Muslim respect for these other religions is a form of self-respect—as the man said, one cannot hate Jesus and be a true Muslim.

Stressing the common elements does not mean that the differences among the religions should be denied or dismissed. Each religion has its own unique understanding of the nature of God, and each has developed a particular language for describing the divine-human relationship. To ignore those divergences would be foolhardy and irresponsible. The intent here is to balance the scale. While the differences are well documented and known by many, the similarities are sometimes unacknowledged. Here, they will be brought to the surface and their implications will be considered.

MUSLIM BELIEF

In the previous chapter, some of the basic practices of Islam were identified and discussed. The similarities among Muslims, Christians, and Jews regarding how they outwardly express what they believe should be readily apparent—followers of all three religions profess their faith, engage in prayer, provide for those in need, practice fasting, and journey to sacred sites. The same interconnections can be noted when we turn to orthodoxy, the content of belief. In general terms, there is a great deal of overlap among the three religious systems regarding what their followers are expected to profess and believe. The Qur'an has a succinct statement of the essence of Muslim faith in 4:136: "Whoever does not believe in Allah, His angels, His books, His messengers, and the last day has strayed far." These five articles of faith are the theological basis or framework for the activities that make up the five pillars treated earlier.

1. ALLAH

As mentioned in the previous chapter, Islam considers the unity and oneness of Allah (*tawḥīd* in Arabic) to be the defining quality of the deity. This is seen in the first half of the profession of faith ("There is no God but Allah") that is repeated three times during every call to prayer, and it is a theme that is repeated throughout the Qur'an—"Truly, your God is one" (37:4). The most serious sin a person can commit is to engage in *shirk*, associating something else with Allah in a way that violates the divine unity. *Shirk* can take different forms, including polytheism, the worship of idols, or ascribing divinity to someone or something in the created world. According to the Qur'an, it is the only offense that will not be pardoned by God. "Surely, Allah will not forgive having something associated with Him, but He will forgive anything short of that as He pleases. Whoever associates something with Allah has committed a grave sin" (4:48).

The ninety-nine names of Allah that were discussed earlier describe attributes of the one God, but they do not go against the monotheism that is at the heart of Islam. Allah remains totally transcendent and other for Muslims, but aspects of the divine nature are revealed through these attributes. In the same way, the many Qur'an texts that have Allah speak in the first person plural form ("We," "Our," etc.) do not reflect the existence of more than one God. They are simply an example of the use of what is sometimes called the "divine we," a more exalted form of discourse that is found in other texts, including the Bible. For example, in the creation story in the book of Genesis God says, "Let us make humankind in our image" (Gen 1:26). The use of the plural in reference to God is also sometimes understood as reflecting the ancient belief that the deity has a heavenly court in which angels and other supernatural beings are present and do God's will. For example, the creation story in the Qur'an describes a scene in which God tells the angels to bow down before Adam (7:11; 15:28–30).

One of the most important qualities associated with God for Muslims is mercy. This is seen in the Qur'an passage cited above that states Allah will forgive any sin short of *shirk*.

God's boundless mercy far exceeds humans' capacity to do wrong, and any sinner's offenses can be forgiven. Time and again in the Qur'an human beings fail to submit themselves fully to the divine will, but as long as they express their remorse and acknowledge their error they are pardoned by God. For example, when Adam and Eve disobey in the garden and eat the fruit of the tree that God prohibited from them, they admit their mistake and God forgives them (7:23). Islam's emphasis on the mercy of Allah is seen in the fact that all 114 chapters of the Qur'an but one (the ninth chapter is the lone exception) begin with a statement that calls attention to it: "In the name of Allah, the merciful, the compassionate."

Perhaps no other text encapsulates the Muslim understanding of Allah better than the first chapter of the Qur'an, called *al-fātiḥah* ("The Opening"):

> In the name of Allah, the merciful, the compassionate.Praise to
> Allah, Lord of the universe, the merciful,
>> the compassionate,
>> Master of the day of judgement.
>> You alone do we worship, and You alone
>> do we ask for help.
>> Guide us along the straight path.
>> The path of those You have favored,
>> not of those who have incurred Your
>> anger nor of those who have gone astray.

This brief chapter, which is recited frequently by Muslims, identifies some of the major roles God plays in Islam: creator, judge, object of worship, helper, and guide. The Muslim

(literally, "one who submits") is to surrender to the divine will
so that he or she may be among those rewarded by Allah
and therefore avoid the fate of those who are punished. The
image used in this opening chapter of the Qur'an to describe
how they should conduct their lives is that of "the straight
path," a term that is synonymous with Islam and mentioned
often elsewhere in the text.

A final aspect of the Islamic view of the deity that non-
Muslims should be aware of is that this is the same God
as the God of the Bible. Throughout the Qur'an and other
Islamic sources, this fact is asserted and highlighted. "He
(Allah) has revealed to you the book (the Qur'an) in truth and
confirmation of what came earlier. He revealed to you the
Torah and the Gospel before this as a guide for humanity"
(3:3). At times, Jews and Christians have claimed that the
God of Islam is not the God they follow, but that is not how
Muslims see things. Due to the belief noted earlier that the
deity has delivered the message of submission many times
throughout history to various prophets, most of whom are
biblical figures, Islam teaches that the God of the Qur'an is
the biblical God. This is the main reason why Muslims have
respect for Jews and Christians—the same God has spoken to
all three groups.

2. ANGELS

The second tenet of Muslim faith is the belief in angels. As the
following *hadīth* illustrates, angelic beings figure prominently
in the early sources:

Abu Huraira reported that Allah's Messenger said, "When it is Friday, the angels stand at every door of the mosque and record the people in the order of their arrival. When the Imam sits to deliver the sermon they fold up their sheets and listen for the mention of Allah."

Angels often play a role in Islam similar to what is found in Judaism and Christianity, where they function primarily as messengers for God. A prime example of this is Gabriel, who Muslims believe to be the intermediary through whom Allah revealed the Qur'an to Muhammad. Gabriel is mentioned by name three times in the Qur'an, where he and Michael are identified as chiefs among the angels (2:97–98; 66:4). Although he is not explicitly named in the passages, Islamic tradition maintains that Gabriel told Mary she was pregnant with Jesus in the Qur'an's accounts of the event (3:45–47; 19:16–21).

A number of Muslim ideas about angels have no basis in the classical Islamic sources. One example of this is the belief in guardian angels, whose job it is to protect people, and who are greeted on one's left and right during prayer. Similarly, there is a popular belief in the existence of Munkar and Nakir, two angels who visit the dead in their graves and question them about their faith and commitment to Islam during their lives.

Islam makes a distinction between angels and another category of supernatural beings called *jinn* (singular, *jinni*), from which the English word genie is derived. The relationship between the two groups is not completely clear in the Qur'an and other sources. In pre-Islamic times, the *jinn* were spirits found in the desert and other parts of the natural world that were hostile to humanity. In Islamic thought, they have the capacity to interact with humans in ways that can both help them and harm them. Perhaps the most prominent angelic being in the Qur'an is also identified as a *jinnī* in one text. "When We said to the angels, 'Prostrate yourselves before Adam,' they all prostrated except Iblīs. He was one of the *jinn* and neglected the command of his Lord" (18:50). Because he refuses to bow down to Adam, Iblīs the "fallen angel" is expelled from the heavenly ranks. The name Iblīs is most likely an Arabic form of the Greek word *diabolos*, from which the English term "devil" comes. In the garden story Iblīs is identified as Satan, who deceives Adam and Eve into eating the forbidden fruit (7:19–25). The fact that Iblīs is referred to as both an angel and a *jinnī* (as well as Satan) is one reason why the difference between the two categories is not entirely understood.

3. BOOKS

Belief in the books is the third element of Muslim faith. Islam is a classic example of a revealed faith—it asserts that it has received revelation in the form of a text from a divine source that provides its adherents with guidance on how to conduct their lives. Islam does not claim to be the only revealed religion because it maintains that other previous peoples have also been the recipients of a divine message. "Truly, this is a revelation from the Lord of the universe. The true spirit has come down with it upon your [Muhammad's] heart so that you might be a warner in clear Arabic language. It was also found in earlier writings" (26:192–96).

This passage states that the message of the Qur'an was also communicated in prior scriptures. As mentioned above, the Torah and the Gospel are the two texts commonly identified as having the same origin as Islam's sacred book (Qur'an 3:3). In other words, the revelation found in Judaism and Christianity is of the same source and nature as that of Islam. The Qur'an even refers to the Torah and Gospel as possessing "guidance and light" (5:44–46). This is a primary reason why Jews and Christians are to be respected by Muslims as People of the Book (see below)—they, too, enjoy the privilege of being recipients of Allah's message.

The Islamic view of the previous scriptures, however, is not an entirely positive one. Muslims believe prior texts like the Bible were corrupted because errors and inaccuracies were introduced into them. These distortions were not the work of Moses and Jesus, the prophets who received the revelations. Rather, they are the fault of their followers, who did not faithfully preserve the message in its original form. This necessitated the sending of another text, the Qur'an, that accurately records Allah's will for humanity and sets the record straight.

Consequently, the Bible in its current form is of both divine and human origin. Where its message coheres with that of the Qur'an, it is authentic revelation. But those places where it disagrees with it are evidence of tampering. For example, any passages in the New Testament that ascribe divinity to Jesus are considered to be texts that do not accurately reflect God's message for humanity. The Qur'an does not explicitly level the charge of distortion against the Bible, but it can be inferred in a number of places. For example, the Islamic text calls itself a clear book, free of doubt and error, that is meant to be guidance for all humanity. "These are the verses of the clear book. We have sent down an Arabic Qur'an so that you might understand" (12:1–2). The implication in this and many similar passages is that the prior books lacked the qualities of clarity and reliability found in this one.

Despite this critique, however, Islam's recognition of the value of the earlier revelations should be kept in mind. Note that the article of faith mentioned in 4:136 is in the plural form ("books"), not the singular. While the Qur'an enjoys special status as the final revelation from Allah, previous messages to humanity also merit respect and honor. Some have suggested that other sacred writings beyond those in the Bible should be included among the books that Muslims should revere, but this has been a matter of some debate. This idea has been proposed for the scriptural texts of Zoroastrianism, a religion with a monotheistic message that began in the area of modern-day Iran and has very few followers today but traces its roots back more than three thousand years. It is quite likely that members of the early Muslim community would have come in contact with Zoroastrians and their sacred scripture, known as the Avesta, and so it is not inconceivable that it is one of the writings included in the Qur'an's injunction to believe in the books.

4. MESSENGERS

The fourth article of Muslim faith is belief in messengers. Islam makes a distinction between the office of the messenger (*rasūl*) and that of the prophet (*nabī*), but the difference between the two is often not completely clear. The term "messenger" is mentioned more than three hundred times in the Qur'an, while there are approximately seventy-five occurrences of the word "prophet." One passage states that the Qur'an does not name every messenger who lived (40:78), and there is a tradition that claims that there were 315 messengers and 124,000 prophets throughout history before Muhammad. As noted earlier, it is frequently said that the messenger, unlike the prophet, is given a book and functions as a lawgiver. But this contrast does not appear to be supported by the Qur'an. For example, according to the Qur'an God gave David the book of Psalms, but David is never described as a messenger in the text.

The individuals identified as messengers in the Islamic text are Noah, Lot, Ishmael, Moses, Shu'aib, Hūd, Ṣāliḥ, Elijah, Jonah, Jesus, and Muhammad. Several of these figures are also found in the Bible, while others (Shu'aib, Hūd, and Ṣāliḥ) are only known from the Qur'an and were probably Arabian prophets of the pre-Islamic era. These three non-biblical messengers are never referred to as prophets in the Qur'an. Among the messengers, Moses, Jesus, and Muhammad are the only ones who were given a book. Of the others, only Noah can plausibly be considered a lawgiver, so this does not appear to be the proper basis on which to distinguish messengers from prophets.

A more accurate distinction that is supported by the Qur'an is that messengers, unlike prophets, are sent to a particular people to serve as figures of authority. "For every nation there is a messenger. When their messenger comes matters are decided equitably among them and they are not wronged" (10:47). This explains why another common English translation of *rasūl* is "apostle," a term that highlights their role as envoys but should not be confused with the Christian meaning of the word. The disciples of Jesus are mentioned several times in the Qur'an, but they are never referred to as "messengers." The prophets, on the other hand, are sent to preach to or warn people, but do not have the same leadership function that messengers have. There are more prophets than messengers mentioned in the Qur'an, and among them are the biblical characters Abraham, Isaac, Jacob, Aaron, David, Solomon, and Job. Most of the prominent prophets of the Bible, like Isaiah, Jeremiah, Amos, and Hosea, are not mentioned in the Islamic sources. According to the Qur'an, some messengers, like some prophets, rank higher than others (2:253)—this is likely a reference to those who are mentioned specifically in the text—but at the same time people should not make any distinctions among them (2:136; 4:150–52).

Muhammad is called both a messenger and a prophet in the Qur'an. He is the quintessential messenger in the text (7:158; 48:29), and the phrase "God and his messenger" in reference to him occurs almost ninety times in the book. Because his message faithfully communicated Allah's will for humanity, there is no need for another to come after him. For this reason, he is referred to as the "seal of the prophets" (33:40). He is the final link in a chain of individuals sent by God that stretches back through history. His connection with these prior figures is explained in the directive given to him in Qur'an 3:84: "Say, 'We believe in Allah, what has been revealed to us, what was revealed to Abraham, Ishmael, Isaac, Jacob, and the tribes, and what was given to Moses, Jesus, and the prophets from their Lord. We do not make a distinction among any of them and to Him we submit.'"

Jews and Christians should keep in mind that Muslims revere some of the very same figures they themselves hold up as models of faith, and that the Islamic belief in messengers implicitly acknowledges the worth of the other monotheistic religions. According to the following *ḥadīth*, Muhammad taught his followers to remember the messengers on a daily basis:

> Al-Bara' ibn 'Azib reported that Allah's Messenger (may peace be upon him) commanded a person, "When you go to bed at night, you should say, 'O Allah, I surrender myself to You and I entrust my affairs to You with hope in You and fear of You. There is no resort and no deliverer from hardship but You. I affirm my faith in the book that You revealed and in the messengers whom You sent.'"

5. THE LAST DAY

The belief in the last day is the fifth article of Muslim faith. There will be much upheaval at the end of the world that will usher in the day of judgment, when each person will be held accountable for the way he or she lived and will be either rewarded or punished for eternity. In the words of the Qur'an, it will be "[a] day on which people will be like scattered moths and the mountains like fluffy wool. The one whose deeds weigh down the scale will have a peaceful existence. But the one whose deeds rise in the scale will have the abyss as an abode. Do you know what that is? It is a scorching fire" (101:4–11). Nearly seventy of the Qur'an's chapters comment on some aspect of the last days. The text is often vivid in its depiction of what will happen at the end of time, but it lacks a comprehensive account of the events. Other Islamic sources, like exegetical writings, *hadīth*, stories of the prophets, and works devoted to eschatology, develop and expand upon the Qur'an passages to create an ordered framework of what will happen in the final days. Among the signs of the end times mentioned in these texts are smoke, the beast, the deceiver, sunrise in the west, earthquakes, and fire.

In the oldest Qur'an passages, the most common way of identifying the end times is with the expressions "the day of resurrection," which is found seventy times, and "the day of judgment," which appears thirteen times. In later texts, the phrase "the last day" is used approximately twenty-five times, and other ways the Qur'an refers to the end times include "the hour," "the day of decision," and "the day of reckoning." The last phrase relates to one of the ninety-nine names of God—"the One who reckons." The Qur'an does not identify when the last judgment will occur or where it will take place, but it will be final and irrevocable.

The Qur'an contains a number of graphic descriptions

of heaven and hell. Paradise is a place of flowing streams and lush gardens, where the good are rewarded with companionship, cool drinks, and delicious food. "Here is what the garden promised to the pious is like—it has rivers of unpolluted water, rivers of milk that never spoils, rivers of wine that is delicious for those who drink it, and rivers of pure honey. They will have every kind of fruit and forgiveness from their Lord" (47:15). Hell is the antithesis—a place of unbearable heat, where its inhabitants are surrounded by fire and forced to drink boiling liquids while experiencing unspeakable tortures. "If the unbelievers only knew the time when they will not be able to keep the fire from their faces and their backs, and they will receive no assistance" (21:39).

Islam stresses personal responsibility and sees the day of judgment as something each individual must experience on his or her own. The idea did develop, however, that Muhammad is able to function as an intermediary who can plead before Allah on behalf of a person being judged. This belief arose as a result of interpretation of the passage, "No one may intercede with Him (Allah) except with His permission" (10:3). In some Islamic traditions Jesus, too, will have a role to play on the day of judgment. On the last day, people will be judged on the basis of how well they submitted themselves to the will of God. One Qur'an text speaks of each group of people being held accountable to its own standards, and it suggests that non-Muslims can be saved:

> You will see each community kneeling and each one called to
> its book. That day you will receive your recompense for what

you have done. This, Our book, will speak about you in truth, for We have recorded in it everything you did. Those who believed and performed good deeds will gain admission into His favor by their Lord. This will be a clear reward. As far as those who did not believe—was My message not read to you? You have been a conceited and sinful people. (45:28–31)

THE PEOPLE OF THE BOOK

The similarities between Islamic beliefs and those found in the other monotheistic religions should be obvious. One all-powerful God, angelic beings, revealed texts, prophetic figures, and a judgment day are all part of the belief systems of most Jews and Christians. These connections are acknowledged by the Islamic sources, and this has led to a special status for Judaism and Christianity in the eyes of Muslims.

This status is best expressed by the phrase "People of the Book" (*ahl al-kitāb*), which is found frequently in the Qur'an. There is some debate regarding the groups that comprise this category, but all scholars include Jews and Christians as People of the Book. As noted above, some would add Zoroastrians and followers of other pre-Islamic religions as well. In the Qur'an and other sources, the People of the Book are spoken of in both positive and negative terms. The phrase "People of the Book" appears some thirty times in the Qur'an. In places, they are privileged because they are the recipients of the divine word, and are therefore viewed more favorably than non-Muslims who practice polytheism or other forms of false worship. The verse found at the beginning of this chapter reflects this more positive view—Jews and Christians are encouraged to follow the teaching found in the Torah and Gospel.

Elsewhere, a more critical tone is adopted when the People of the Book are discussed, with some texts differentiating between good individuals and bad individuals within the group:

> If the People of the Book had believed and been pious We would have granted pardon for their offenses and allowed them to enter the gardens of comfort. If they had followed the Torah and the Gospel and what was sent down to them from their Lord, they would have eaten of good things from above them and from under their feet. Among them are some who are moderate, but many of them do evil. (5:65–66)

The majority of passages that do not make a distinction among the People of the Book are critical of them, with a common complaint being that they do not recognize the validity of Muhammad and his message. Such passages need to be read and interpreted within their proper theological and historical contexts. The Muslim understanding of revelation sees the Qur'an as the definitive word of God that had to be sent because all previous scriptures are distorted and incomplete. It is therefore not surprising that people who continue to use those prior writings are criticized in the Islamic sources. Similarly, the circumstances of Muhammad's life and his interaction with the People of the Book, particularly Jews, contributed to a negative assessment of them. We have seen that the early *ummah* experienced some tension with the Jewish community at Medina, and this undoubtedly influenced Muslim attitudes toward them.

The presence of similar material in their revealed texts is an indication of the special relationship between Muslims and the People of the Book. While not adopting the chronological format of the Bible, the Qur'an contains many references to individuals and events found in the biblical text. Stories associated with six main biblical figures are present throughout Islam's sacred text: Adam, Noah, Abraham, Moses, Mary, and Jesus. Abraham and Moses are the two most frequently cited individuals in the Qur'an, and Mary, the mother of Jesus, is the only woman mentioned by name in it. In addition, the story of Joseph, the son of Jacob who was sold to Egypt by his brothers, is told in chapter 12 of the Qur'an in the longest single narrative the book contains.

This biblically related material can give the Qur'an an air of familiarity for the Jewish or Christian reader at first, but the differences soon become apparent. The stories are never recounted in precisely the same way that they are found in the Bible, and the Islamic text contains material not present in the Jewish and Christian scriptures. In general, there is a tendency to Islamize the biblical figures so that they fit the Muslim context and reflect the concerns of the Qur'an. In this way, the Qur'an is consistently engaged in the process of interpreting the biblical tradition for its audience.

Another difference that is immediately apparent to the Bible reader is the way the Qur'an is organized. Large sections of the biblical text follow a fairly clear chronological order: it begins "in the beginning" with the book of Genesis and traces the experiences of the Israelites through the various periods of their history. This same approach continues in the New Testament where the story of Jesus' life is told in narrative form in the gospels, and this is followed by the story of the early church as presented in the Acts of the Apostles.

The Qur'an is structured according to a completely different principle. Its 114 chapters are presented by order of length, with the longest chapters followed by the shortest ones. The first chapter is quite brief and functions as an introduction to the entire book. It is followed by chapter 2 which, at 286 verses, is the Qur'an's longest. By contrast, chapter 108 is only three verses in length. Counting the pages in a recent English translation of the Qur'an can help show how this ordering affects the book's structure—if we divide it in half, the first 57 chapters of this translation take up 374 pages and the last 57 chapters need only 84 pages, and many of those in the second half contain only a few lines of text.

We see a good example of the differences between the Qur'an and the Bible in the way Noah is presented. It often escapes the attention of Bible readers that Noah has only one line of dialogue as his story unfolds in Genesis 6–9. It is found at the very end of the section, when he curses the offspring of one of his sons and blesses his other two sons (Gen 9:25–27). In the period prior to the flood and during the deluge itself, the biblical Noah does not utter a single word. In the Qur'an, on the other hand, he has much to say. Noah speaks constantly as he goes about the process of warning his contemporaries of the impending flood unless they change their ways and worship the one true God (11:25–49;

71:1–28). The reason for this difference is simple. Noah is a prophet in Islam, and prophets must speak in order to exercise their office. He is therefore given a voice that is almost totally lacking in his biblical counterpart. There are numerous examples of this type of Islamization of biblical characters throughout the Qur'an.

The biblical personage that presents the most problems and potential for misunderstanding is the Qur'an's treatment of Jesus. He is a central figure in the text and is unique in many ways—Jesus is virginally conceived by Mary, and he is acknowledged as the Messiah who is able to perform miraculous works that are beyond the capabilities of others (3:42–51; 19:2–36). He is one of only a handful of people who have been entrusted with a written message for his people. There is much about Jesus that sets him apart and makes him greatly admired by Muslims.

The problem is that Islam flatly denies the divinity of Jesus, an essential belief of Christianity. "They have disbelieved who say, 'Truly, Allah is the Messiah, the son of Mary'" (5:17). Jesus himself even refutes the claim that he is divine. In one text, after Allah asks him if he has ever told his followers to take him as a god, Jesus responds, "Praise be to You! It is not for me to say that of which I have no right. If I had said it, You surely would have known it. You know what is in my mind, but I do not know what is in Your mind. You are the knower of hidden things" (5:116). In this and several other passages, the Qur'an rejects the beliefs in the Trinity and the incarnation that are central to Christian faith.

It can be painful, even insulting, for Christians to read

a text in which the founder of their religion denies the cornerstone of their faith. As valid as this initial reaction might be, it is important that Christians try to understand the basis for Islam's view of Jesus. Here, too, they need to consider the theological context in which such ideas are found. Islam is insistent in its critique of Jesus' divinity because it is an example of *shirk*—to say that Jesus shares in God's nature is to associate a created human being with the uncreated deity in a way that violates the divine unity.

It is highly unlikely that Muslims and Christians will ever see eye-to-eye or reach common ground on some very important issues like this one. Perhaps the most that can be hoped for is a mutual willingness to agree to disagree in a spirit of tolerance and respect for the view of the other. The theological differences between them regarding Jesus are significant and long standing, but in many other areas of their faith lives Muslims and Christians, along with Jews, have much in common. This can be a good starting point from which to attempt to develop a relationship based on trust and openness.

RESPECT AND THE NON-MUSLIMS

It would be a serious error to assume that Muslims are taught to hate Jews and Christians, and that they perceive these groups to be their enemies. There is no ingrained animosity toward Judaism and Christianity imbedded in Islam. Just the opposite is true. The followers of Moses and Jesus enjoy a special relationship with Muslims since they have all been given the same revelation. This is summed up succinctly in the Qur'an passage that reads, "Certainly, some from among the People of the Book believe in God" (3:199).

An example of Muslim respect for members of the People of the Book can be seen in the "A Common Word" initiative of 2007. In September of 2006, Pope Benedict XVI gave a lecture in his native Germany that contained a reference to Islam that many people considered to be inflammatory and that led to strong negative reactions from Muslims and non-Muslims alike. In October of the following year, more than one hundred Muslim leaders from around the world signed a letter that was addressed to the pope and other Christian leaders inviting them to recognize and celebrate two things that Muslims and Christians have in common—love of God, and love of neighbor. The name of the initiative comes from a verse in the Qur'an that begins with the words, "People of the Book! Come to a common word between us and you" (3:64). The document elicited positive responses from many on the Christian side, and it resulted in a number of meetings and conferences between Christians and Muslims that have led to improved relations and a greater appreciation of what unites members of the two religious traditions. The Common Word initiative was a clear example of how, even under trying circumstances, a positive outcome is possible when people respond in a spirit of respect.

This is not to say that there have been no problems since then. As is often the case among people of different faiths, religion has sometimes been a tool used by all three monotheistic communities in order to support theological, political, and social agendas. All parties must do what they can to avoid this and establish relationships that are tolerant of the differences among them.

But this work must begin at home—we can each only take care of our own side and try to improve the situation there. In this effort, Jews and Christians would do well to keep in mind the deep respect most Muslims have for their religions and the potential this offers. Within Islam there is an inherent appreciation of the worth of the People of the Book that can be validated and sustained by Jews and Christians. If they live good lives that are in conformity with the teachings of their sacred texts, they will have justified and earned the respect of Muslims.

QUESTIONS FOR DISCUSSION

1. What do you consider to be some of the main obstacles to positive relations among Jews, Christians, and Muslims?
2. Where do you see some of the best opportunities for positive relations among them?
3. What are the most important similarities among the three monotheistic religions? What are the most important differences? Are the similarities or the differences more significant?
4. What things can Jews and Christians do to earn the respect of Muslims?
5. Visit the Common Word website to read the document and some of the responses to it (http://www. acommonword.com). Can this initiative serve as a useful

model for future efforts at dialogue between Muslims and non-Muslims?

4

There Is No Institutional Hierarchy in Islam

O believers! Obey Allah and obey His messenger and those in
authority among you. When you disagree among yourselves
on some matter, refer it to Allah and the messenger if you
believe in Allah and the last day. That is a good thing and the
best of outcomes.

—Qur'an 4:59

One of the questions often asked by non-Muslims in the
wake of events like the attacks of September 11, 2001 or
the beheadings of innocent people by ISIS usually goes
something like this: "If Muslims disagree so strongly with
what Osama bin Laden, ISIS, and other terrorists have done
in the name of Islam, why don't they do or say something
about it?" On the surface, this may seem to be a logical and
simple question, but it is not as easy to answer as it might first
appear.

For a community to take a unified stand on an issue, it

helps if there is some established body or organization that can discuss the matter, render a verdict, formulate a response, act as a mouthpiece, and pronounce a statement. A recognized and agreed-upon authority, whether an individual or an assembly, that can function as a spokesperson is one of the quickest and most effective means of communicating a group's position to a wider audience. Such an organizational structure is sometimes found in religious communities, with one of the clearest examples being the Catholic Church. When the pope or a synod of bishops issues an encyclical or other statement that is widely published and disseminated, it is generally believed to contain the official Catholic teaching on a matter.

This kind of structure does not exist in Islam, where there is no clergy or institutional hierarchy, and non-Muslims are often unaware of how leadership and authority function in the religion. It has already been noted that the *imām* plays an important role in leading communal prayer in the mosque, but this office is different from that of the priest, minister, or rabbi. The prayer leader in Judaism and Christianity is usually someone who has an advanced degree in theological studies and whose special status in the community is recognized through the ritual of ordination or in some other official way. This is not necessarily the case for the *imām*. He may have formal training in Islam—in large mosques this is usually so—but he is not required to have this background. Similarly, there are no formal bodies of *imāms* who are organized by geography or denomination that function as groups analogous to what is commonly found in Christianity and

Judaism. Leaders of Islamic communities tend to operate independently, and only on occasion do they join together to act as an assembly in an official capacity.

A rare exception to the decentralized state of affairs within Islam described above can be found in Iran, where the Shi'i leadership of the country forms a recognizable and vocal group with its own hierarchy that often speaks with one voice. Hierarchy is understood in different ways depending on which branch of Shi'ism is being considered, but the form it takes in Iran will be the focus here since it is probably the most familiar example for non-Muslims. One's position in the religious hierarchy of Iran is determined by the individual's educational background, with Ayatollah being the most well-known title among the country's religious elite. Less commonly known is the fact that there are several levels both below and above that of Ayatollah, with those above it having titles that translate as "Grand Ayatollah," "Source of Imitation," and "Highest Source of Imitation." Each of these levels is achieved through outstanding contributions to both society and the scholarly community, and as one rises through the religious ranks one's social status is also enhanced because religious leaders play a key role in Iranian political life. After the Iranian Revolution of 1979, Ayatollah Khomeini instituted a new system in which Shi'i clergy have *de facto* final authority over the country's parliament. The Supreme Guide, a position he held until his death in 1989, is at the top of the pyramid of Iran's political system, and Ayatollahs and other members of the clergy hold key posts in the various councils and assemblies that come under the Supreme Guide's authority.

Outside of Iran, such a hierarchical ordering of religious leaders is unknown in Muslim-majority countries, and this is partly due to the Islamic concept of *ummah*. It reinforces the idea that Muslims comprise one community that is united in its faith, and no distinction is to be made among the membership on any basis. The presence of a clergy that could be set apart and placed above other Muslims would be counter to the egalitarian spirit that is central to their faith.

Another reason why a hierarchical system has not developed within the Islamic community is a theological one. The Muslim is one who fully submits himself or herself to Allah's will. God alone, and no one else, should be obeyed and followed. A framework with levels of authority like that found in some other religions runs the risk of creating a situation in which one might have to express obedience to another human being, thereby violating the command to submit oneself only to Allah.

This lack of centralized authority in Islam has both strengths and weaknesses. On the positive side, it can encourage a more democratic sense within a religious community. A feeling of equality among all members is easier to achieve when there is no chain of command in which those at the top exercise power and control over those below them. An expression of this can be seen in Qur'an 3:103, where the *ummah* is presented as a family of faith: "Hold on to the rope of Allah all together and do not become divided. Remember Allah's favor upon you when you were enemies of each other. He joined together your hearts so that by His favor you became brothers and sisters." According to this passage, Muslims are siblings who are yoked to the "rope of Allah," an interesting image that will be discussed in more detail below.

Despite the benefits that a lack of hierarchy might bring to a religious community, such an arrangement can lead to problems. One of the most vexing challenges facing Islam today is related to an issue addressed earlier—who speaks for the group? Without a structure in place to facilitate the process of formulating and communicating an official position on an issue, it can be difficult to answer this question definitively. Do all Muslims speak for Islam? If so, what happens when they disagree on a matter and there is no clear consensus? Does difference of opinion on certain matters suggest that there can be no "official" view? Should some Muslim voices be taken more seriously than others? These and similar questions have become more pressing with the creation and proliferation of various forms of social media that have been used by extremist Muslims and their groups to promote their messages, publicize their activities, and recruit new members. These individuals and organizations have grown increasingly savvy about how to use modern technology for their own purposes, with the result that they can now instantaneously communicate with a much larger audience. This sometimes complicates efforts to determine what the authentic voice of Islam is.

This situation is particularly crucial when the issue at hand is a controversial one that has an impact on the lives of people outside the *ummah,* as was the case after September 11, 2001 and on similar occasions when Muslims engage in acts of violence that they attempt to justify on religious grounds. At such times many non-Muslims are looking for a statement endorsed and agreed upon by the Muslim community that would denounce terrorist attacks and articulate Islam's official reaction to the events. Such a statement is often not forthcoming because there is no central authority that is able to coordinate the effort to formulate and communicate it. But this does not mean that authority is lacking in Islam and that Muslims are free to do what they wish in the name of their faith. On the contrary, the Islamic community has a very well developed sense of the nature and structure of authority that will now be considered.

ISLAMIC LAW

Allah is the supreme authority in Islam. By acknowledging the complete power of God and surrendering oneself to the divine will, a person performs the perfect act of submission (*islām*). The *ummah* is a community whose members freely submit themselves in this way and are united under the authority of Allah as brothers and sisters. This is the message behind the text cited above from Qur'an 3:103—Muslims should all hold on to the "rope of Allah" in order to maintain their unity.

According to Arabic dictionaries, the term *rope (ḥabl)* can have a number of different meanings. It can refer to a cord that is used to tie or bind something, but it can also be used to express the nature of certain relationships. Sometimes it describes a covenant or bond that exists between two parties that have particular obligations and responsibilities toward one another. In several places in the Qur'an it is used in this way, and that appears to be its sense in this passage. According to 3:103, Muslims receive divine favor in the form of a united community by holding fast to the rope of Allah. This rope is what joins all Muslims together, and it is also the means of approach or access to Allah. It is what allows Muslims to be aware of God's presence and will in their lives. In this way, the "rope of Allah" is what connects a Muslim to both God and the other members of the *ummah*.

The Qur'an passage at the beginning of this chapter (4:59) also underscores Allah's authority for Muslims. Directed to believers, it tells them they should obey Allah, His messengers, and those "in authority among you." It then goes on to say that when matters of disagreement arise among them they should consult Allah and the messenger. This text presents a kind of pecking order of authority for Muslims—they should listen first to Allah, then to the messenger, and finally to those in authority. One of the ways in which Allah's authority is most fully realized is through Muslim obedience to God's law. The chain of command in this passage is an outline of how law functions in Islam. It comes from Allah, is found perfectly expressed in the life of the Prophet, and is communicated by legal scholars, those "in authority among you." In this way, the law functions as the rope of Allah that unites all believers and gives them access to God's will for them.

The Arabic term for law, *sharīʿah*, is well known to many non-Muslims but is not commonly found in the classical Islamic sources. It appears only once in the Qur'an (45:18), where it does not have the meaning "law" but rather conveys the basic sense of "path, road." The verse is directed to Muhammad, and it warns him against being swayed from the direction that God has laid out for him. "They placed you on the path (*sharīʿah*) of the command, Follow it, and do not follow the whims of those who do not know." Similarly, the word *sharīʿah* and terms etymologically associated with it are found only about a dozen times in the *ḥadīth* material, and only one of these occurrences can plausibly be given a meaning related to law. This indicates that the use of the term *sharīʿah* with reference to Islamic law postdates the time of the Prophet Muhammad. In fact, scholars agree that the Islamic legal system is the result of a developmental process that took place over centuries.

Islam spread rapidly in the generations after Muhammad when Muslim thinkers in different parts of the world began to establish the framework of Muslim jurisprudence or *fiqh*, the academic discipline in which scholars study *sharīʿah*. Eventually, there emerged four main schools that continue into the present day. Each of the four schools is named after its founder: Mālik ibn Anas (d. 795), Abū Ḥanīfa (d. 767), al-Shāfiʿī (d. 820), and Aḥmad ibn Ḥanbal (d. 855). Of these four men, al-Shāfiʿī is generally considered to be the most influential because he was the one who systematized the Islamic legal system and refined its methodology. These are the four schools that are recognized within Sunni Islam, while Shi'i law developed its own legal system by drawing upon sources unique to it and relying upon the authority of leaders like the Ayatollahs.

Each area or country in the Sunni Islamic world follows one or more of the four schools of law. The differences among the schools are usually not profound, but the way they use the legal sources can sometimes lead to varying interpretations and rulings.

There are four sources for Islamic law, and they recall the admonition discussed above to obey God, messengers, and those in authority. The first is the Qur'an itself. If the sacred text takes a clear and unambiguous position on a legal matter, it must be followed. An example of this is the prohibition against fornication in 17:32. "Do not go near adultery. It is immoral and an evil act." Non-Muslims often assume that Islam's sacred text contains many laws, but that is not the case. In fact, the Qur'an contains very little explicitly legal material—some scholars say the designation applies to fewer than seventy of the book's approximately 6,300 verses.

The *hadīth* material is the second source of law. Muhammad is considered to be the ideal Muslim, and so traditions that report what he said and did have played a significant role in the development of the Islamic legal tradition because they serve as models of proper behavior. This is an area in which some disagreement among schools can be seen. The Ḥanbalī school, popular in Arabia, tends to rely on the *hadīth* a great deal, while the Ḥānifī school, which has the largest number of followers throughout the world, is a bit more speculative and is not as dependent on the prophetic traditions.

The third source is consensus, or *ijmāʿ*. If the first two sources are not helpful in determining a legal ruling, one can appeal to the consensus of the community. This practice is based on a prophetic tradition in which Muhammad said, "My community will not agree on an error." This has proved to be a controversial matter at times because there is some question regarding who is to be consulted. According to al-Shāfiʿī it originally referred to a consensus of the Muslim community at large, but this soon became impossible for logistical reasons and over time it has come to refer to the opinions of the religious scholars alone.

Analogy, or *qiyās*, is the final source of Islamic law. If a question cannot be resolved through use of the first three sources, one can compare the debated point with another one analogous to it in order to reach a decision. A frequently cited example of this concerns the consumption of whiskey. The Qur'an and *ḥadīth* collections make no reference to it, but they do prohibit the drinking of wine (Qur'an 5:90–91). Since whiskey has similar properties and effects to those of wine, Muslim legal scholars argue analogously that drinking whiskey is also banned in Islam.

A point of contention among Muslim legal experts has been the permissibility of *ijtihād*, the use of one's independent reasoning, in forming legal opinions. Those who are more conservative maintain that all one needs to do is consult the classical legal sources of Islam and apply their content to any situation regardless of the context. Others believe a degree of independent reasoning is necessary in order to determine what in the Qur'an and *ḥadīth* material is relevant for later periods and what is not. Reformers like Muhammad Abduh, who will be discussed later, fall in this latter category. The most liberal of scholars argue that *ijtihād* should be given free rein in order to bring Islam into the modern world.

This is such a hotly debated issue because in the tenth century it was claimed that the "door to *ijtihād*" had been closed for good and personal interpretation was no longer necessary because Islamic law had reached a fully developed stage. This led to an ossification of the legal tradition, which some argue needs to be rejuvenated by reopening the "door to *ijtihād*." Others disagree and say the practice of law should be nothing more than the repetition and application of long established principles and methods.

As noted earlier, the schools of law mentioned above are found only in the Sunni branch of the *ummah*. Shi'i Islam has its own legal tradition that is in many ways quite similar to that of the majority group. Some of the most important differences can be seen in the sources and methodology employed. The *ḥadīth* literature is a source for Shi'i law as well, but the body of traditions consulted is somewhat distinct. The Shi'i community has a large number of *ḥadīth* that trace their roots to Ali and his successors in the Imamate and are not a part of the Sunni corpus, but figure prominently in Shi'i jurisprudence. Another difference can be seen in the frequent use of *ijtihād* by Shi'i scholars, for whom this is a less controversial issue.

Islam has a vast body of legal literature that covers many different areas. Some of it concerns matters that pertain to the faith lives of Muslims, like prayer and fasting. Other laws deal with issues related to interpersonal relations, including marriage, divorce, inheritance, debt, and crime. In its totality, Islamic law covers virtually every aspect of human behavior, and some Muslims think it should be applied as broadly as possible. This is an issue of debate within Islam that is often misunderstood by non-Muslims. While some Islamists, extremists in particular, would like to see *shari'ah* as the law of their land, this is a minority opinion that does not have a great deal of popular support. In recent times, people in the United States have sometimes expressed concern that Islamic law might somehow become a part of the American legal system, and some states have attempted to prevent this from happening by proposing legislation that would ban official recognition of *shari'ah* law in US courts. Whatever the motivations of such initiatives, they reflect a lack of awareness about the nature of Islamic law and how it functions in the everyday lives of Muslims. Depending on how the legislation were written, to ban *shari'ah* outright could have the unintended consequence of rendering illegal central Islamic practices like prayer and fasting during the month of Ramadan.

Islamic law has been adopted as the official legal code in some places like Saudi Arabia and Iran, but most countries in the Islamic world have instituted a system that combines Islamic law and civil law. Typically, Islamic law is applied only to family matters like marriage, divorce, and inheritance, while the civil courts decide other cases, including criminal law.

The lack of a centralized authority or hierarchy in Islam has influenced how law is practiced. When a judge (*qāḍī*), who is often appointed by the state, desires a legal opinion (*fatwā*) in order to reach a decision, he will consult a legal scholar for guidance. Each scholar operates independently by using the methodology of a particular school to formulate an opinion. If the judge, or some other individual consulting the scholar, is dissatisfied with the legal ruling, another scholar who might offer a different opinion on the matter may be consulted. The term that is often used to refer to the body of legal scholars in a given area or throughout the Islamic world is '*ulamā*' ("learned ones").

A *fatwā* is only a personal opinion that is not legally binding, but sometimes one will be issued without being requested in order to respond to some important matter or to influence public opinion. One of the most well-known *fatwās* of recent times was that issued by Ayatollah Khomeini in 1989 against the British–Indian author Salmon Rushdie, whose controversial novel, *The Satanic Verses*, the Iranian leader and others considered to be an insult to Islam. The *fatwā* labeled Rushdie a traitor to Islam and called for his death. Another prominent *fatwā* was the one issued by Osama bin Laden against the United States in 1998 that will be discussed in a later chapter.

The punishments that are prescribed in the Qur'an for certain crimes are familiar to most non-Muslims. Perhaps the one that is best known is amputation of the hands of those caught stealing (5:38). Other punishments, called *ḥudūd*, mentioned in the Islamic text include execution by crucifixion or the sword for robbery with homicide (5:33), and flogging for less severe unlawful sexual intercourse, false accusation of unlawful sexual intercourse, or drinking wine (24:2). The Qur'an does not prescribe stoning for adultery, but this form of capital punishment is mentioned in the *ḥadīth* literature. Such punishments are carried out on occasion in a few places in the Islamic world, like Saudi Arabia, but they are extremely rare. Since *sharī'ah* is applied only in matters pertaining to family law in most countries, those places do not enforce the penalties listed in the Qur'an for criminal offenses. Non-Muslims should therefore avoid judging Islam based on some of the punishments found in its sacred text. Most Muslims prefer to interpret them contextually as appropriate for seventh-century Arabia but not relevant for modern society. This is similar to how most Jews and Christians view many of the punishments for various offenses that are found in the Bible, like the command that children who curse their father or mother should be put to death (Exod 21:17).

Even though *sharī'ah* does not govern every aspect of a person's life in most Islamic countries, Muslims have no doubt about its importance. The law is the "rope of Allah" that unites the *ummah* and leads its members to God. It is therefore not accurate to say there is no centralized authority in Islam.

There is no *human* centralized authority in Islam—all power is centered and resides in Allah.

GENDER RELATIONS

The lack of an institutionalized hierarchy in Islam also has an impact on gender relations, an area about which non-Muslims often have preconceptions that are not completely accurate. In the view of many, Islam is a very patriarchal, even misogynistic, faith that privileges men and oppresses women. One of the most common images associated with Islam is that of a veiled woman dressed in loosely fitting clothes who lacks freedom and a voice to speak her mind. The pictures that were broadcast around the world of women dressed in this manner after the Iranian revolution of 1979 and, more recently, from Taliban-controlled Afghanistan and parts of the Middle East under the authority of ISIS have helped to perpetuate this stereotype.

Non-Muslims must be careful to avoid generalizations about the entire religion when they see such images. Here, as elsewhere, the diversity and complexity of Islam must be kept in mind. Men and women relate to each other in a variety of different ways throughout the Islamic world, and it would be a mistake to universalize the situation in one place by applying it to all Muslims. This is not to deny that women are oppressed and treated unfairly in some Islamic countries. Such situations certainly exist, but they do not reflect the circumstances of all Muslim women. The experience of women under regimes like that of the Taliban or ISIS is markedly different from that in some parts of North Africa, for example, where women and men usually relate as equals.

This aspect of the religion highlights the critical role that interpretation plays in determining what is acceptable or required in Islam. The lack of an overarching authority or ruling body that could articulate the official Muslim position on the role of women means that legal scholars in each area, working individually or collectively, consult the sources and apply the principles of the methods they have adopted. Those who believe they should exercise independent reasoning (*ijtihād*) to interpret the ancient sources in light of the modern world will likely reach conclusions different from those who reject the use of *ijtihād* and prefer to simply apply the sources literally to a later context. A consideration of what the early sources have to say about key aspects of male-female relations underscores the importance of the interpretive process.

In places, the Qur'an communicates an egalitarian and positive message about the relationship between men and women by stating that they are created equal and meant to live together in harmony. "It is He (Allah) who created you from a single cell, and from it created its mate, so that he might rely upon her" (7:189). In 4:124 no distinction is made between men and women when it comes to rewarding those who act properly. "Whoever does good works, whether male or female, and is a believer—they will enter heaven." Elsewhere, women are to receive the dowry owed them in marriage (4:4), and, like men, they are entitled to a share of the inheritance left by their parents and other relatives (4:7). Throughout the Qur'an, the obligations and duties of men and women are identical, and they will all be rewarded in the same way if they carry out those responsibilities (9:71–72). Elsewhere, unbelievers and sinners are sometimes discussed in the same way with no distinction made among them on the basis of their gender (9:67–68). One of the Qur'an's most tender descriptions of the bond that exists between spouses is found in 30:21, which states that each partner should be a source of security, support, and trust for the other. "Among His signs is that he has created spouses for you from among yourselves so that you might find comfort in them. He put love and compassion between you. There truly are signs in this for a people who reflect." Such texts have caused many commentators to describe the ideal view of the relationship between men and women in Islam's sacred book as one of equality and parity.

Other passages draw a distinction between men and women that favors the male. For example, in 2:282 the number of witnesses necessary to verify a legal transaction is given as two men or one man and two women. The text then states that two women are necessary because if one forgets what she has seen or becomes confused the other can remind her. Similarly, according to the opening words of 4:11 male heirs are entitled to receive twice the amount of inheritance that female heirs receive. "God commands you concerning your offspring: for the males, a share equal to that of two females."

Verses like these need to be read and interpreted within their original contexts. There is no denying that, in places, the Qur'an is a patriarchal text that tends to privilege the male perspective. Such texts reflect the cultural norms and practices of its era and place—the society of seventh-century Arabia was male-dominated. These passages present women in the way they do because the world of business transactions and financial matters was primarily the realm of males, and women were, for the most part, unfamiliar with it. The text that stipulates that two women attend a legal proceeding attempts to ensure that the outcome is fair and just, but it is not making a negative comment on their mental capacities. It is simply acknowledging a sociological fact of the time—the world of business and commerce was a male-centered one with which women had relatively little experience and familiarity. Similarly, the passage regarding inheritance is speaking to a context in which males were expected to be the source of financial stability in the family, and therefore brothers were provided with more resources than their sisters when their parents died.

The presence of texts like these in the Qur'an that seem to privilege men over women raises important questions that are at the heart of the reader's interpretive process as he or she tries to determine their meaning and relevance. Should these passages be literally applied to the present day and therefore shape our understanding of what the roles of men and women should be? Or should the present-day reality of those roles inform our understanding of the texts? The decentralized nature of religious authority in Islam makes both approaches possible, and there are many examples of each throughout the Muslim world. Those in favor of the second approach maintain that it is important to distinguish between two different types of texts within the Qur'an and other Islamic sources. The first are those passages presenting an egalitarian view of male/female relations that expresses Islam's dominant perspective, and are therefore relevant for all times and places. The second are texts that do not put both groups on equal footing, but favor men over women. Such texts are context-specific and relevant only for the unique circumstances of seventh-century Arabia, but they have nothing to say to us in the modern world because they express an understanding of gender relations that does not reflect our own. According to this approach, it is only texts of the first type that should be consulted in our day and age, and the others should be ignored. Here again the similarities with how Jews and Christians read the biblical literature are obvious because many of them choose to disregard those parts of the Bible that are misogynistic or in conflict with contemporary views of how men and women should relate to one another.

How best to interpret texts that oppress and marginalize women is an issue that the *ummah* must continue to wrestle with and attempt to address. The literal application of the entirety of the Qur'an and other classical sources to the modern context is something that has led to a considerable amount of tension and controversy within the Islamic community. Many are of the opinion that too much reliance upon and application of the legal system as formulated in the medieval period causes a great deal of harm to Islam and stifles its creative spirit. This is a matter that will be addressed in the next chapter in the discussion of recent Islamic movements like modernism and reformism.

Islamic teaching concerning polygyny and divorce has been a subject of interest to non-Muslims. Qur'an 4:3 allows men to have up to four wives, and throughout history Muslim men have been married to more than one woman at the same time. Non-Muslims need to keep in mind, though, that this is a relatively rare practice in most of the Islamic world and some countries have actually outlawed multiple marriages. Some scholars argue that the Qur'an itself places a virtual ban on the practice. After permitting up to four wives, the text of 4:3 goes on to say that if a man thinks he cannot treat all of them equally he would do better to marry only one woman. Later in the same chapter, 4:129 states that this is an ideal that is impossible to achieve. "You will not be able to act justly with your wives no matter how much you desire to do so." Many commentators think that this denial of the possibility of being impartial in a situation of multiple marriages is a virtual abrogation of the other verse (4:3) and therefore nullifies the practice of polygyny. At the very least, 4:129 expresses a strong preference for monogamy and discourages marriage to more than one person.

Divorce is a complex issue in Islam, partly because the Qur'an is not completely clear on the process to be followed. Although it is permissible to divorce, Islamic teaching clearly views marriage as a lifelong commitment that should be broken only in exceptional situations. This sentiment is expressed in a ḥadīth that has the Prophet Muhammad say,

"Of all the things permitted to a Muslim, divorce is the most abominable in Allah's eyes."

The Qur'an asks Muslim men either to keep their wives with honor or to release them with honor (65:2), and this led to the development of several different types of divorce within Islamic law. One form has the divorce take effect three months after the man states, "I divorce you." The three-month waiting period is mentioned in the Qur'an (2:228) as a way of both establishing the paternity of any offspring should the woman be pregnant and allowing for the possibility of reconciliation between the couple. During the waiting period, the man must provide for the woman and allow her to stay in the house. Here, too, one reason for their close proximity is the hope that they will be able to repair the damage to their relationship and remain married, although the primary motive is the support and protection of the woman and her offspring (65:6). A variation on this has the man say, "I divorce you," once in three successive months. The couple can resume a normal married state at any point during those three months, but at the end of the period the divorce is final if they have not done so. According to the Qur'an, a divorce is considered official when, after the waiting period, it is proclaimed in the presence of two witnesses (65:2). The third type of divorce goes against the Qur'an's command to wait three months and allows the man to utter the words three times in succession, making the divorce effective immediately. Women have the right to initiate divorce in Islam, but the process usually entails presenting her case before a court. The precise requirements differ among the legal schools; but the most common grounds upon which a woman can file for divorce include desertion, impotence, and insanity on the part of her husband.

The final area to consider is that of women's dress. It often comes as a surprise to non-Muslims that only two passages in the Qur'an explicitly treat this issue. The first is found in 24:31. "Tell the believing women to lower their gaze and guard their private parts. They should not display their beauty except that which is normally exposed, and they should cover their breasts with their veils." The text goes on to mention those members of a woman's household before whom this requirement might be relaxed. The basic message is that women should dress modestly in public and avoid calling undue attention to themselves. Interestingly, the opening words of this verse are found in the one before it, this time directed toward believing men who are told to lower their gaze and guard their private parts. In this way, the Qur'an's vision of equity between the genders extends to the matters of dress and public decorum.

The Qur'an's other reference to women's dress is in 33:59, which is directed to Muhammad and reads, "O Prophet, tell your wives, your daughters, and women believers to have their outer garment hang low over them. That way, they will be recognized and not be harassed. God is forgiving and merciful." The verse does not describe the garment in any detail, but it is not referred to as a *ḥijāb*, the usual word for a veil. It is important to note that the verse makes it clear that the purpose of the garment is not to cover up the women or render them invisible. Just the opposite is the case since it is meant to make them visible to others, especially non-Muslim men, by serving as a marker of their status as Muslim women that protects them from unwanted advances.

Non-Muslims often assume that the practice of a woman donning a veil is something mandated in the Qur'an, but that is not the case. The word *ḥijāb* is found seven times in the text, but in none of those cases does it refer to an article of clothing that is meant to cover some part of a woman's (or man's) body. Rather, they all describe some kind of barrier or partition that forms a separation between those on one side of it and those on the other side.

It should be noted that nowhere does the Qur'an call for the full covering of women. The ḥadīth and other sources suggest that during Muhammad's lifetime only his wives wore veils, as seen in the expression "she took a veil," which meant a woman had become the Prophet's wife. Study of neighboring cultures indicates that veiling of women was practiced in Syria and Palestine, but it is unknown precisely how it spread to the Islamic world. Most likely, it was assimilated into Islam from areas that were converted by the early community.

In very few places in the modern Islamic world are women completely covered from head to toe. When they are, it is usually because they are required to dress in this manner. In such cases, we see examples of men exercising authority over women in a way that denies them freedom of choice. Various other types of veiling are commonly found throughout the *ummah*. Westerners sometimes consider the modified veil that covers the head but leaves the face exposed to be a symbol of the oppression of Muslim women. When they do so they may be misinterpreting matters. Muslim women wear veils for a variety of reasons, many of their own choosing. In some places they are required to do so by law or by order of those in power. But elsewhere many women speak movingly of the free choice they have made to wear a veil as a symbol of their identity as Muslims and their commitment to their faith.

HIERARCHY AND THE NON-MUSLIMS

The lack of a clergy and a clearly defined hierarchy in much of the Islamic world has sometimes caused non-Muslims to misinterpret the views and thoughts of members of the Muslim community. This is especially true when, as in recent times, violence is done in the name of the religion and non-Muslims look for an Islamic decree from on high or a completely united front that does not materialize. Some non-Muslims then reach the mistaken conclusion that Muslims, including their leaders, actually approve of terrorism or that Islam is by nature a violent religion. Nothing could be further from the truth. In fact, many Muslim individuals and groups have spoken out against those who try to justify terrorist acts by appealing to Islam, and their voices have been particularly loud since the tragic events of September 11, 2001. Links to many of these statements that denounce terrorism can be found at the following website: http://kurzman.unc.edu/islamic-statements-against-terrorism/.

When those reactions by Muslims are deemed insufficient or insincere, the fault usually lies with the non-Muslim expectations, not the Muslim responses. The organization and structure of the *ummah* is not conducive to the formulation and communication of a statement that would speak for all Muslims everywhere. The same thing might be said of Christianity—imagine the chaos that would result if the non-Christian world asked for a pronouncement that would reflect the "Christian view" on some important matter!

Non-Muslims need to recognize that Muslims are addressing the problem of violence in their own way. They are just not doing it in the way some non-Muslims would like to see it done. This is a problem that non-Muslims, not Muslims, have to acknowledge and address. They can begin to do so by realizing that there are many ways that religious communities can organize themselves and attempt to communicate their views to both members and non-members. A system that is appropriate for one group should not become a yardstick by which to measure the effectiveness of another.

QUESTIONS FOR DISCUSSION

1. What are the advantages and disadvantages of having a religious hierarchy? What are the advantages and disadvantages of not having one?
2. How would you compare Islam's understanding of authority with that of other religious traditions with which you are familiar?

3. Is the use of independent reasoning (*ijtihād*) an essential part of being a person of faith in the modern world?
4. What should determine whether or not a person is a legitimate spokesperson for his or her religion?
5. What might non-Muslims do to become more receptive to Muslim efforts to speak out against violence done in the name of their religion?

5

There Is No Clear Separation between Religion and Politics in Islam

If God appoints someone as ruler over a people and he dies
while he is treacherous to his people, God will forbid his entry
into Paradise.

—The Prophet Muhammad

It has been noted already that there is a close connection
between religion and politics in Islam that can be traced to
the earliest days of the religion. When Muhammad accepted
the invitation to serve as a judge for the people of Yathrib
(later Medina), it was expected that they would acknowledge
his religious authority as well. This is reflected in the
"Constitution of Medina," a document mentioned earlier that
outlines the relationship between the newly arrived Muslims
and the inhabitants of Medina. It states, "Whenever a dispute
or controversy likely to cause trouble arises among the people
of this document, it shall be referred to God and to

Muhammad, the apostle of God. God is the guarantor of the pious observance of what is in this document."

Because the practice of the Prophet is typically seen as the ideal to be emulated and a model to follow, later generations of Muslims have often sought to make sure that their religion continues to be engaged with the political sphere in their own day. This is an aspect of Islam that non-Muslims need to be aware of since it provides important background for understanding certain developments and events in recent times. Many of the stories related to Islam that have captured the world's attention during the past few decades have had a political component to them. Among the places where this has been the case are Iran, Turkey, Algeria, Kashmir, Indonesia, Israel/Palestine, Afghanistan, Iraq, Tunisia, Libya, Syria, and Egypt.

This is an issue that has engendered a fair amount of debate within the *ummah* itself—the nature of the relationship between religious belief and political concerns is not something on which all Muslims agree. While some call for a complete separation of the two, many Muslims maintain that Islam needs to have a voice in the political arena. The difference of opinion usually concerns the amount of influence Islam should exert and how that influence should be expressed. This general acceptance of religious input in political discourse is related to the topic treated in an earlier chapter that Islam is a religion of orthopraxy. True faith must be articulated in action, and this will inevitably put it in conversation with the political reality. The *ḥadīth* at the beginning of this chapter succinctly sums up the standard

Muslim view of the relationship between the two areas—a political leader who is not a good Muslim will not be rewarded in the hereafter.

The range of perspectives on this matter can be seen in a second report issued by the Pew Research Center discussing the results of their survey that was mentioned in an earlier chapter. (That report is available here: www.pewforum.org/files/2013/04/worlds-muslims-religion-politics-society-full-report.pdf.) According to the survey, regional differences exist regarding the role of religious leaders in politics. The majority view among Muslims in South Asia, Southeast Asia, North Africa, and the Middle East is that religious leaders should have, at a minimum, at least some influence in politics. At the same time, this was the minority view among those surveyed in Central Asia, Southern Europe, and Eastern Europe.

For some non-Muslims, the events of the "Arab Spring" in 2011 were an illustration of the nexus between politics and religion that exists within Islam. The popular demonstrations that were held throughout the Middle East at that time led to the overthrow of a number of regimes that had been in power for long periods of time, most notably in Tunisia, Egypt, and Libya. Religious figures and rhetoric played some role in those outcomes, but it would be a mistake to view them as Islamic revolutions. Leaders like Hosni Mubarak in Egypt and Muammar Ghaddafi of Libya were forced out for many social, political, and historical reasons that had very little to do with religion. In some places, religious ideas or sentiments might have helped to fan the flames, but their downfalls were primarily due to the dictatorial styles of governing they adopted that alienated them from their people. Mubarak was initially replaced by someone affiliated with an Islamic group, as will be discussed below, and this might have reinforced the perception that the Egyptian revolution was primarily religious in nature, but this is a misreading of what actually happened.

To say that there is a close connection between religion and politics in Islam is not to say that every Muslim political leader has religious authority and vice versa. This has been true in some periods and places throughout history, but it is rarely the case today. For example, the political system present in post-revolution Iran since the late 1970s gives the country's religious authorities a great deal of political power and influence, but this is more an exception than the rule in the modern world. Nonetheless, in many Islamic societies faith is expected to inform and shape the area of politics. This is a very complex aspect of Islam that can be treated only superficially here. In this chapter, we will briefly consider some of the important figures that have been involved in efforts to put Islam in conversation with political concerns, and some recent examples of the connection between religion and politics.

ISLAM AND WESTERN INFLUENCE

By the mid-nineteenth century there was a very strong European presence throughout much of the *ummah*. The position of power and prestige that Islam had enjoyed for centuries had begun to give way as European states more aggressively asserted themselves in other parts of the world. This shift was due to a number of factors. One of the most important was the high level of technological advancement and scientific knowledge present in Europe, which surpassed what was available in the Islamic world. This led to improvements in military and administrative capabilities that allowed the Europeans to expand their sphere of influence and move into areas of the globe previously off-limits to them. By the early-twentieth century virtually every Muslim country was either under direct colonial rule or a protectorate of one of the European powers.

Responses to this situation varied. Some, particularly those who benefited financially or politically from the Western presence, were able to tolerate the new arrangement more easily. Others saw the colonial powers for what they were—outsiders who were exploiting the resources of the conquered territories for their own selfish purposes with little regard for the concerns of the local populations. The fact that these newcomers were non-Muslims raised a number of important questions. Is this permissible under Islam? Should non-Muslims be ruling Muslims? Should they be tolerated or overthrown? Why has Islam lost its influence in the world? A number of Islamic movements emerged in the attempt to answer such questions. Two of the most important are modernism and reformism, which are associated with Ahmad Khan and Muhammad 'Abduh, respectively.

MODERNISM

The modernist holds the view that in the encounter between

Islam and new ideas or contexts the religion must often adapt if it is to maintain its relevance. In other words, Islam should be transformed or changed in order to fit the new circumstances, rather than vice versa. When this is applied to a political issue, like Western presence in Islamic countries, it means that Muslims should somehow modify their understanding of their faith in light of what they learn from their interactions with Europeans.

Ahmad Khan (1817–98) was a prime example of a modernist. He lived in India during a period of British rule, and he strongly advocated the adoption of Western ideas and institutions. He was particularly influential in the field of education as the founder of the Muhammadan Anglo-Indian College at Aligarh, where European arts and sciences were taught in English along with Islamic studies.

Khan was strongly influenced by the European Rationalism of the nineteenth century, and he believed Islam needed to be reinterpreted in order to reflect modern systems of thought. For example, he accepted Darwin's theory of evolution, and this put him at odds with Islamic scholars. His view on evolution served to further complicate his standing in the community because he already had an uneasy relationship with most Muslim authorities due to his insistence that Islam should be reformed. One element of the religion of which he was especially critical was the role of the *ḥadīth* material. Khan dismissed all of the prophetic traditions as spurious and unreliable, and he was vehemently opposed to consulting them for assistance on how to live as a Muslim in the modern world. As already discussed, this attitude toward the *ḥadīth* was shared by other Muslims who viewed them cautiously. But because of his high profile as a reformer, Khan became a lightning rod for those who did not share his perspective on the matter.

One of the most controversial aspects of Khan's approach was what he called the "criterion of conformity to nature." He saw no inherent contradiction between the word of God as revealed in the Qur'an and the work of God as found in the natural world. Here, too, he held a position that was shared by many of his fellow Muslims, who thought that both the Qur'an and the world reveal something about God. Where he parted ways from many of them, though, was in his understanding of the relationship between the two. According to Khan, the truth of Islam or any other religion can be determined by how well it conforms to nature. When there is a contradiction between what one's religion teaches and what nature teaches through reason and the senses, one should accept the latter and reject the religious teaching as untrue. This caused him to discard much of the Islamic legal system as an archaic institution that did not relate to modern concerns, and to call for the removal of other components of the religion that, in his mind, were nothing but relics and vestiges of the past. At the top of his list of things that should be abandoned was what he considered to be an overreliance on the *ḥadīth*.

Khan's high regard for the West is quite apparent throughout his writings. He sought to remove the contradictions between traditional Islam and modern science, and he believed the best way for the Muslims of India to do this was to accept British rule and adopt a more European perspective on the world. He called for a passive stance before the foreign powers that would ultimately bring about a positive change in Indian society and establish a better, more modern form of Islam.

REFORMISM

Ahmad Khan was an extreme modernist who attempted to respond to European influence through a process of adaptation intended to westernize Islam. Others opted for a more moderate approach that preferred to accept only those ideas and aspects of Western culture that did not compromise their Islamic identity. These individuals recognized that the tendency to rely upon and cling to the past (*taqlīd* in Arabic) that had characterized Islam for centuries was a problem that needed to be addressed. They readily acknowledged that Islam needed to change in order to be relevant in the modern world, but they thought the best way to do this was to reform it from within rather than have it changed from the outside, as Khan proposed.

One of the most influential reformers was the Egyptian Muhammad 'Abduh (1849–1905), who was ideally suited for his role. He was a student of Jamal al-Din al-Afghani (1838–97), a highly respected scholar from Afghanistan who stressed the compatibility between Islam and science while fiercely opposing colonialism. 'Abduh was in a unique position to have his voice heard and taken seriously—he was the rector of al-Azhar University, one of the most prominent institutions of higher learning in the Islamic world, the chief judge (*mufti*) of Egypt, and the editor of the important reformist journal *al-Manār* in which he published many of his influential writings.

'Abduh drew a distinction between the essential core of Islam and its general principles. The core is comprised of the doctrines that are the basis of the faith and treat such matters as revelation, articles of belief, and morality. According to 'Abduh, the content of this core is unchanging and relevant for all times and places. The general principles, on the other hand, are adaptable and changeable since they are applied to particular contexts in order to develop laws and social teachings. When the context or circumstances change, the laws and social customs often need to be modified. 'Abduh believed it is the responsibility of Muslim thinkers and jurists to make sure that the changing laws and principles cohere to the unchanging core of Islam. He felt that this was a particularly important task in situations like his own in nineteenth-century Egypt, where Muslims were coming in contact with and being influenced by non-Muslims.

In his efforts to modernize Islam by reforming it from within, 'Abduh pushed for social reform in Egypt through his publications and legal pronouncements. 'Abduh was particularly concerned about issues that affected the status of women, like their lack of educational opportunities and the negative effects of polygamy. He argued passionately that Islam's essential core does not say anything about these matters since they come under the heading of laws or social customs that can be changed to reflect new contexts. Practices that might have been appropriate in seventh-century Arabia should not be blindly imitated and imposed on people living in the modern world. Following this method, 'Abduh went about the task of trying to rid Egyptian society of outmoded ways of thinking and living that, in his view, actually went against the spirit of Islam. In this way, he was a strong proponent of the use of *ijtihād*, or independent reasoning, in order to develop more appropriate ways of being a Muslim in the modern world.

The difference between modernism and reformism should be apparent. Modernists like Ahmad Khan look to the West for guidance on where and how Islam should change. He thought women should be educated because this is one of the marks of a "civilized" society like those in Europe. Reformists, on the other hand, look within Islam to determine how the religion should change. 'Abduh argued that women should be educated because this was one of the marks of an Islamic society in his day, which was markedly different from the context in which the Prophet Muhammad lived in seventh-century Arabia. The difference between the two can also be seen in their attitudes toward the *ḥadīth* collections. While Khan dismissed all of the prophetic traditions as unnecessary, 'Abduh was less extreme. He acknowledged that the *ḥadīth* material could sometimes be a hindrance to modernization, but he accepted those whose reliability was attested by scholars. Here, too, he operated more within the framework of traditional Islam than Khan did.

ISLAM AND SOCIAL ACTIVISM

India and Egypt were also the birthplaces of two important religious groups whose influence has continued into the present day. The Jamaat-i-Islami, founded by the Indian Mawlana Abul Ala Mawdudi (1903–79), and the Muslim Brotherhood, founded by the Egyptian Hassan al-Banna (1906–49), are religious organizations that have often played a political role in the countries where they are found. Both of these men were raised under British rule in areas that had strong anticolonial feelings. Mawdudi and al-Banna were critical of Western influence, and they saw Islam as the solution to many of the problems in their societies.

The founders of the Jamaat-i-Islami and Muslim Brotherhood shared a common vision that was expressed differently in the Indian and Egyptian contexts. They believed that Islam's blend of religious faith, political engagement, and social concern distinguished it from other religions, and that all non-Islamic societies were therefore inferior. The two groups they founded attempt to inculcate within their members an awareness of the social responsibility that goes along with being a Muslim. They are organized in local branches that offer prospective members a period of orientation that imparts religious knowledge and moral instruction. Both the Jamaat-i-Islami and Muslim Brotherhood emphasize the importance of social activism through involvement in youth work, education, health care, publishing, and many other social projects that their members organize and support.

Mawdudi was a journalist who tried to develop a framework for the revival of Islam in India by writing on the connection between Islam and the social issues of his day, like poverty, education, and the role of women. As a theological conservative, he tended to rely on the classical sources of Islam to support his views, and he frequently called for a return to the prophetic ideal as found in the life of the Prophet Muhammad. He founded the Jamaat-i-Islami in 1941 and moved to Pakistan six years later when that Islamic state was created. In his writings and approach, Mawdudi sought to attract the well-educated members of society to join his movement because they were in the best position to bring about the change he desired.

According to Mawdudi, the oneness of Allah (*tawḥīd*) should be the first principle of a political system. Once this is accepted as the basis and starting point of change, a true Islamic state begins to emerge. He believed the perfect form of society is not a democracy as defined by the West, but a "theodemocracy" in which the will of the people comes under and conforms to the will of Allah. The hallmarks of such a system are equity and social justice that allow all members of society to live in peace and prosperity. He turned to Qur'an texts like 22:41 to support his vision of a society in which all people take care of each other under the authority of the one God. "Those whom We establish on the earth observe prayer, give alms, demand what is good, and forbid what is evil. But the final result of all things rests with Allah alone."

Mawdudi's ideas sometimes put him at odds with political

authorities. He and other leaders of the Jamaat-i-Islami have been imprisoned or persecuted on occasion, but the group has generally been allowed to function in society. In addition to India, the movement has also attracted a significant number of members in Pakistan, Kashmir, and Afghanistan.

The Muslim Brotherhood has exerted more influence and has played a bigger political role than the Jamaat-i-Islami. Like the Indian organization, it was formed in response to the perceived threat that the strong Western presence posed and it, too, attempted to address that concern by stressing the need to turn to Islam to combat the problems in society. The movement was begun by Hassan al-Banna in 1928, but since that time its presence has spread far beyond its original Egyptian context and it can now be found throughout the world in places as diverse as the Middle East, North Africa, and Indonesia.

Though its membership initially came from the rural lower and lower-middle classes, the Muslim Brotherhood quickly grew into a mass movement that attracted many professionals who joined its ranks. At one time its members numbered more than one million. By the late 1920s many Egyptians had become disenchanted with the parliamentary structure put in place by the British, and they felt their country was losing touch with its roots. Al-Banna responded to this situation by founding the Muslim Brotherhood and calling for a return to the basics of Islam. In his view, this was a way of combating the westernization and secularization that were threatening the future of his country.

The approach al-Banna adopted was extremely

effective—he translated Muslim faith into social action. The Muslim Brotherhood took the lead by meeting some of the most basic needs of the population in ways that the government did not. They became involved in issues like organized labor, land distribution, and municipal investment, and they helped to staff and run schools, clinics, and soup kitchens. And they did it all in the name of Islam while reminding other Muslims of their responsibility to work toward social reform.

After World War II the Muslim Brotherhood became more overtly political as al-Banna called for an end to foreign occupation and the replacement of secular institutions with Islamic ones. He was assassinated, probably by government agents, in 1949 so he did not see the revolution three years later that gave Egypt its independence. Since that time, the Muslim Brotherhood has had an unsteady relationship with the Egyptian authorities. Although always viewed cautiously by those in power, the organization sometimes has been able to express its views openly and function without any fears. At other times, it has been silenced and forced to go underground as a result of government crackdowns and rulings against it.

During the years that Hosni Mubarak was the President of Egypt (1981–2011) the Muslim Brotherhood was the largest opposition group in the country, and it was sometimes the target of persecution and mass arrests. Although it was not then officially recognized as a political party, the organization scored a stunning victory in the parliamentary elections of 2005, when members of the Muslim Brotherhood who ran as independents captured nearly ninety seats, or 20 percent of the total. Following the Egyptian revolution of 2011 that ousted Mubarak, the group was legalized and began to exert significant political influence. The newly formed Freedom and Justice Party, which was created by the Muslim Brotherhood, won nearly one-half of the almost five hundred seats in the 2011 Egyptian parliamentary elections, more than any other political party. In June of the following year, the Muslim Brotherhood candidate Mohamed Morsi was elected Egyptian President, and he held that position for a little over a year until he was forced out of office by a military coup after growing accusations of corruption and ineptitude within his administration. Hundreds of Muslim Brotherhood leaders and members were arrested in the aftermath, and many of them, including Morsi himself, have been sentenced to death.

As these events demonstrate, the Jamaat-i-Islami, the Muslim Brotherhood, and similar groups share a perspective that often puts them at odds with those who are running their countries. One issue that has caused problems is nationalism. By the 1960s most of the countries in the Islamic world that were under foreign control had won independence and achieved statehood. This development was broadly celebrated, but many Islamists feel the resulting situation is not ideal and is actually sinful. In their view, the existence of numerous Islamic entities goes against the notion of a single *ummah* of Muslims united in their faith. People like Mawdudi, al-Banna, and their successors are willing to tolerate the presence of separate Muslim states as an unavoidable consequence of colonialism, but they see it as a temporary situation that will exist only until the full unity of the community that the Prophet Muhammad called for is achieved. Obviously, this leads to a great deal of tension with those in power who favor the status quo and have personally benefited from their political positions.

This is related to a second issue: members of these organizations sometimes level accusations against political leaders in a way that questions the leaders' commitment to Islam. Some go so far as to declare those in authority to no longer be Muslims because of their statements, actions, or policies. Charging someone with apostasy (*takfīr* in Arabic) is a very serious matter in Islam that can have grave consequences, but some Muslims maintain they are justified in doing so under certain circumstances. When it is directed against government officials, the close nexus between religion and politics in Islam is readily apparent—how a politician discharges the duties of his or her office can determine whether he or she is a member of the Muslim community in good standing in the eyes of some. This idea is reflected in the thought of the next person to be discussed.

ISLAMIC EXTREMISM

In recent times there has been an increase in radical forms of political Islam that are more militant and violent in nature. The findings of the Pew Foundation survey mentioned earlier indicate that this is a major source of anxiety for Muslims around the world. The study found widespread concern regarding religious extremism among those surveyed in North Africa, the Middle East, South Asia, and

Southeast Asia, with at least one-half of the respondents in nearly every country in each of those areas saying they were very concerned or somewhat concerned about extremist organizations. Groups that adopt this perspective are often confrontational in their relationships with local authorities and foreign governments because these powers are viewed as enemies that must be defeated. One of the most important figures in this development is Sayyid Qutb (1906–66), an Egyptian member of the Muslim Brotherhood who is considered by many to be the founding father of modern Islamic extremism.

Qutb was a teacher who wrote a number of articles in the 1940s that were critical of the Egyptian government. The negative reaction they received forced him to go into exile in the United States for three years. During his time abroad, he was shocked by what he considered to be the lack of morality he observed in American society, which he attributed to rampant secularism. His experiences in the West caused Qutb to become more conscious of his Muslim identity and to reach the conclusion that religion should play a critical role in shaping the values and attitudes of a society.

Upon returning to Egypt in 1951, Qutb became a member of the Muslim Brotherhood and quickly rose through the ranks of the organization. In the years just before and after the Egyptian revolution of 1952 he was an advisor to Gamal Abdel Nasser (1918–70), one of the leaders of the revolutionary movement who went on to become Egyptian President. An unsuccessful attempt on Nasser's life in 1954 was blamed on the Muslim Brotherhood, and Qutb was imprisoned for ten years. After a brief period of release he was arrested again and eventually tortured and executed in August 1966.

While he was in prison Qutb wrote his most important book, *Milestones*, which lays out his vision of Islam. It has become a foundational text for Islamic extremists the world over. In this work and his other writings, Qutb calls for the unity of religion (*dīn*) and state (*dawlah*) in order to rectify the problems in modern society. He believed that Western culture had become completely decadent, and that only Islam offered hope for the future. He thought humanity would never be free until it came under the sole authority of Allah. Qutb appealed to the classical Islamic sources like the Qur'an and *hadīth* for support, and he claimed that any political system not based on them is flawed and should be terminated.

Jāhilīyah ("ignorance") was the term Qutb used to describe the situation created by all un-Islamic societies and political systems. He felt that a society based on anything but Islam—be it communism, capitalism, socialism, nationalism, or another religion—keeps its people from gaining true knowledge, and it will ultimately lead them astray. Qutb also criticized as equally ignorant any Islamic government that did not truly follow the religion, and was therefore Muslim in name only. He believed that this was precisely the problem with all "Muslim" governments of his time, including his own. He was particularly critical of the Egyptian revolution, claiming that it did nothing but usher in a new form of foreign presence. He believed a second revolution was necessary in order to topple the current *jāhilī* ("ignorant") system and replace it with a truly Islamic one. Views like this put him at odds with the Egyptian authorities and ultimately cost him his life.

By choosing the word *jāhilīyah* to define the problem, Qutb framed the situation in theological language. It is a term commonly used in Islam to describe Arabian society prior to the time of Muhammad's prophetic career. People in the pre-Islamic period were in a state of ignorance because they worshipped many gods and did not follow the will of the one true God. Muhammad changed that by bringing the message of the Qur'an and freeing people from their ignorance. Qutb thought the societies of his day were guilty of *shirk* ("association") because the people who were exercising power over others had usurped Allah's authority and set themselves up as false gods.

Qutb believed the perfect Islamic society was that of the Prophet's time, when all Muslims submitted themselves to God and came under the authority of one person who fully submitted himself to the divine will. He further believed that the Prophet wanted this form of government to be re-created by Muslims in subsequent generations. He therefore viewed anything that did not fit this model, whether it comes from the West or from within Islam itself, as an innovation and threat that should be removed.

Qutb was not the first to denounce the Muslim leaders of his time as un-Islamic or to call for a return to the way things were done during Muhammad's time. Ibn Taymiyya (1263–1328) was a very prominent theologian whose views on these matters have influenced many later thinkers, including Qutb. He was a legal scholar who spent most of his life in Damascus and Cairo, and he was extremely critical of the Mongol rulers who had overrun Baghdad in 1258 and brought an end to the 'Abbasid Period. By devising a method for labeling someone an unbeliever and apostate (*takfīr*), Ibn Taymiyya was able to argue that the Mongols were not true Muslims despite their conversion to Islam. He was also very opposed to some of the practices and ideas that had crept into Islam through Sufism and other sources, and he worked hard to expel them. He looked to Qur'an passages like 4:171 to justify his intolerance of innovation—"Do not exceed the limits of your religion." The high regard Muslim extremists like Qutb have for Ibn Taymiyya can be seen in the fact that many of them refer to him simply as "the teacher of Islam" (*shaykh al-islām*).

It would be hard to overestimate the influence Sayyid Qutb has exerted in the modern Islamic world. He took the ideas of previous thinkers like Ibn Taymiyya, Hassan al-Banna, and Mawlana Mawdudi and applied them to his own context in a way that has spoken to later generations of Islamic radicals. His idea that Islam must play an aggressive role in the world in order to combat the forces of evil has become the cornerstone of virtually all extremist groups. Some of the most violent Islamic organizations have justified their activities through his ideology. Among them are Gamaa Islamiyya (Islamic Group), Takfir wal Hijra (Excommunication and Migration), Salvation from Hell, Muhammad's Youth, and Islamic Jihad, the group behind the assassination of Egyptian President Anwar Sadat in 1981. In addition, the Islamic Resistance Movement (better known by the acronym of its Arabic name, Hamas), responsible for much terrorist activity in the Palestinian/Israeli conflict, is the militant arm of the Palestinian branch of the Muslim Brotherhood and therefore traces its roots to Qutb. Among those who have acknowledged Qutb's influence on their thinking are Ayatollah Khomeini of Iran, Shaykh Omar ʿAbd al-Rahman (who is in prison for his involvement in the World Trade Center bombing of 1993 in New York City), Osama bin Laden, and the Egyptian Dr. Ayman al-Zawahiri, who took over al-Qaʿida when bin Laden was killed.

In more recent times, other groups have been formed that appeal to the writings and ideas of people like Sayyid Qutb and Ibn Taymiyya to justify their extremist views and acts of violence in the name of Islam. One such group is Boko Haram, founded in 2002, an organization based in Nigeria that has been responsible for the deaths of tens of thousands of people and the flights of millions of others from their homes because of the group's efforts to establish an Islamic state in West Africa. Boko Haram's close connection to the ideology of Qutb and its call to protect Muslims from everything he considered to be antithetical to Islam can be seen in the group's name, which means "Western influence is forbidden" or "Western influence is a sin."

The same thing can be said of another relatively new organization that has claimed responsibility for numerous acts of terrorism and other atrocities that have been denounced by Muslims and non-Muslims alike. The Islamic State of Iraq and the Levant, better known by the acronyms ISIS and ISIL, first caught the attention of the general public in 2014 when it announced its aim of establishing a worldwide caliphate under the leadership of its head, a man named Abu Bakr al-Baghdadi. Since that time, it has embarked on a campaign of terror that has resulted in many deaths and the displacement of countless people who have fled their homelands. By 2015, ISIS had taken over large portions of Iraq and Syria, and it has endangered other parts of the Middle East in its attempt to create an Islamic state in the area. In addition, people elsewhere have been threatened by the group as it has engaged in brazen acts of violence that have included the beheadings of innocent westerners and attacks launched against defenseless targets in Europe and elsewhere. The call by ISIS to reinstate the caliphate and the means by which it has attempted to do so demonstrate the close ties the group has to the ideology of Sayyid Qutb and similar figures. It considers the present time to be one of ignorance, and it believes that Islam holds the key to a better future. Only when all people come under the authority of a newly formed caliphate in an *ummah* that mirrors the one formed by the Prophet Muhammad will its members have realized their goal. Tragically, through their barbaric acts they have shown a complete disregard for the rights of others, including many of their fellow Muslims, and during Muhammad's time this would have excluded them from the very community they seek to reestablish.

POLITICS AND THE NON-MUSLIMS

The way Muslims typically understand the relationship between religion and politics is quite different from the view held by most Americans and other Westerners. The separation of church and state is a concept that is widely accepted in the West, and it is often considered to be the bedrock of a modern and advanced society. Therefore, non-Muslims often become apprehensive or uncomfortable when they are made aware of the important role religion plays in how some Muslims understand and interpret political events at home and abroad.

Occasionally, they reach the conclusion that Muslims are religious fanatics or that their cultures are underdeveloped because they are not able to keep the areas of faith and politics separate and distinct. Terrorist attacks that have been undertaken in the name of Islam have only exacerbated the problem and reinforced this opinion of Islam in the minds of some non-Muslims. Such attacks are usually understood in political terms, both by those who perpetrate them ("The West must be defeated!") and the victims ("Why are they set on destroying our way of life?"). In the midst of the emotional and physical turmoil of dealing with such horrible events, it is tempting to generalize by blaming Islam as a religion that preaches violence and is backward because of its view of the relationship between religion and politics.

If non-Muslims jump to such conclusions it can lead to a distorted understanding of Islam that unfairly lumps all Muslims into categories like "religious fanatic" and "political extremist." History shows that Islam, like all religions, has had its share of such types. But it would be a gross injustice to assign these labels to all Muslims simply because they are an appropriate way to describe a very small number of them. Non-Muslims should also refrain from negative attitudes about Islamic countries because they do not support the same separation of religion and politics found in the West. It is important to realize that not all people think the same way and that what works in one part of the world is not necessarily applicable to people elsewhere.

This relates to the issue of democracy and Islam. Many Western experts assert that the two are incompatible, and that a truly democratic system will never succeed in a Muslim country. It is certainly true that most Islamic regimes are authoritarian and have not been democratically elected. But this is not automatically the fault of Islam. In places like Sudan, Iran under Ayatollah Khomeini, and Taliban-controlled Afghanistan, Islam has sometimes been used in ways that have led to repression, violence, and injustice. The road to democracy will not be an easy one because of the many historical and political obstacles that have to be overcome. Most of these countries are relative newcomers on the world stage after a long time under colonial powers responsible for the authoritarian atmosphere that still permeates them. To complicate matters, the current leadership is often well entrenched by virtue of dynastic succession or military backing, and therefore resistant to change. This was seen in what took place after the Egyptian revolution of 2011 that toppled President Hosni Mubarak.

After a period of chaos he was replaced by Mohamed Morsi, a member of the Muslim Brotherhood who held office for only a year before he himself was ousted. The person behind Morsi's removal and his replacement as President was Abdel Fattah el-Sisi, who had been appointed by Morsi to be the head of the Egyptian Armed Forces and who had risen through the ranks of the military during the Mubarak regime.

Despite these and other challenges, many reformers believe democracy can become a reality in the Muslim world because it is in line with certain practices and ideas that are basic to Islam. For example, there is a long history of establishing consultative assemblies going back to the time of the Prophet Muhammad that has encouraged consultation (*shūrā*) between rulers and their constituencies in later periods. Some have seen this as a model for exploring ways of allowing the voices of the governed to be heard. Similarly, important legal concepts, most notably independent reasoning (*ijtihād*) and consensus (*ijmāʿ*), can be interpreted in ways that highlight their relevance to the issue of democracy in Islam. The many political rallies and demonstrations for human rights during the Arab Spring of 2011 were a clear indication of the desire for more democratic systems throughout the Muslim-majority world, and the results of the Pew Foundation survey support that conclusion. In thirty-one of the thirty-seven countries where the question was asked, more than one-half of Muslims held the opinion that a democratic government, rather than one that has a leader with a strong hand, would be better able to address the problems facing their countries. Most reformers are quick to point out that an Islamic democracy will not look like a Western one, and this is important for non-Muslims to keep in mind. If a truly Islamic democratic system is to emerge, it must be allowed to do so in its own way and time. To expect it to mirror what is found in the United States or elsewhere, or to question its validity if it does not do so, would be a mistake.

QUESTIONS FOR DISCUSSION

1. What parallels can you draw between the Islamic movements discussed in this chapter and those found in other religions?
2. Do you think the Western presence in the Islamic world was ultimately a positive or a negative experience for those involved?
3. Can violence done in the name of religion ever be justified?
4. What is your reaction to the idea that Islam and democracy are compatible?
5. What is the best way to respond to someone who expresses concern over the relationship between religion and politics in Islam?

Jihād Does Not Only Mean "Holy War"

We have returned from the lesser *jihād* to the greater *jihād*.
  —The Prophet Muhammad

The word *jihād* is familiar to virtually all non-Muslims, but very few of them know its proper meaning. It is an essential and complex concept in Islam that means much more than simply "holy war." Sometimes referred to as the sixth pillar of Islam, *jihād* comes from an Arabic root (*jahada*) whose primary sense refers to the act of putting forth effort in order to achieve some goal. Another word that has already been discussed and comes from the same root is the legal term *ijtihād*, which describes the effort to employ independent reasoning in Islamic law.

THE TWO TYPES OF *JIHĀD*

The term *jihād* occurs only four times in the Qur'an, but

words etymologically associated with it are found about forty times in the text. Analysis of these occurrences suggests that they should be grouped under two main headings. In the first place are those texts that describe the effort each person must exert in order to live as a good Muslim. Like Judaism and Christianity, Islam is keenly aware of the presence of sin in the world, and it urges its followers to be on guard against it. Muslims must therefore do all they can to follow the straight path and to avoid the temptation to do wrong. Some Qur'an passages, like 22:77–78, urge followers to strive daily to put forth the constant effort that this entails:

> O, you who believe! Bow down and prostrate yourselves and worship your Lord. Do good deeds so that you might enjoy success. Strive in the way of Allah with a striving worthy of Him. He has chosen you and placed no hardship upon you in faith, the faith of your father Abraham. He has called you Muslims earlier and in this [book] so that the messenger might be a witness for you and you might be witnesses for humanity. So engage in prayer, pay the almsgiving, and remain devoted to Allah. He is your master—what an excellent master and excellent helper!

The sentence "Strive in the way of Allah with a striving worthy of Him" describes the effort that is demanded of Muslims. The Arabic word translated as "striving" is *jihād*, one of its four occurrences in the Qur'an. The passage makes it clear that an internal, spiritual effort is being called for. The references to bowing, praying, almsgiving, and devotion all highlight the personal faith of the Muslim who is urged to act as one who has been chosen by Allah. In this and similar passages, *jihād* is a concept that cannot be linked to violence or war in any way. The other three Qur'an passages that contain the word *jihād* are 9:24; 25:48–52; and 60:1, and not one of those texts explicitly endorses violence since they describe the inner resolve a true believer must possess that allows him or her to remain faithful. According to these passages, *jihād* is an attitude one must adopt in order to overcome challenges and obstacles that can come from different directions. They could be family members, wealth, or possessions that compete for one's attention and allegiance (9:24; 60:1), or they might be unbelievers who cause one to forget that God is the supreme authority (25:52). Other Qur'an texts containing words derived from the Arabic root *jahada* that do not have a violent connotation include 16:110; 29:69; and 49:13–15.

The second group of words speaks of a different kind of striving that refers to the effort necessary to expand and defend the Islamic community. The originating context of these passages must be kept in mind. It has been noted that Muhammad often met opposition from local leaders in Mecca and elsewhere as he tried to spread the message of Islam. At times his audience was hostile in its response to his attempts to convert them to monotheism. The Qur'an addresses this situation with words meant to strengthen and encourage the Prophet and the early *ummah* not to give up in the effort to bring Islam to their contemporaries. Using words related to *jihād*, a distinction is often made between those who strive in the way of Allah by actively going out and trying to spread the faith, and those who passively stay at home and do not get involved. "Those who believed and left their homes and strove in the way of Allah, and those who sheltered them and helped them—these are the true believers. Forgiveness and a noble provision are theirs" (8:74).

Passages like this one speak of a type of *jihad* that is more external and aggressive than the first group that was mentioned. The expansion of the faith, as we have seen, required warfare and military activity against those who were unreceptive or hostile to the message brought by Muhammad and his followers. Islam, like Christianity and other religions, has had a bloody history at times. Sometimes the threat was of a physical type, rather than spiritual. In those cases, the concept of *jihad* was used to describe the appropriate response to attempts to harm or destroy the *ummah*. This view of *jihad* is present a number of times in chapter 9 of the Qur'an, which has the title "Repentance." Warfare is a theme in several sections of this chapter, and striving or struggling is often mentioned in them. When discussing people who violate their oaths and seek to remove the Prophet Muhammad as their leader, 9:14–16 indicates that *jihad* can take the form of an armed struggle when the community is under attack. The association with violence and warfare is more explicit a bit later in the chapter in 9:38–41, where the people are chastised for not fighting and then warned of the consequences if they continue to refuse to engage the enemy. As these and other passages make clear, violence is appropriate only when it is a defensive response to an attack on Islam or Muslims. One of the most frequently cited texts in this regard is 2:190–92:

Fight in the way of Allah against those who fight you, but do not exceed the limits. Truly, Allah does not love those who exceed the limits. Kill them where you find them, and expel them from where they expelled you. Oppression is worse than killing. Do not fight them near the Sacred Mosque until they fight you there. If they fight you, fight them. That is the reward for unbelievers. But if they desist, surely Allah is forgiving and merciful.

The sentence, "Kill them where you find them," is sometimes read out of context by both Muslims and non-Muslims, creating the impression that Islam supports indiscriminate murder and bloodshed. This is to ignore the rest of the passage, which repeatedly stresses the need for the response to be defensive and to last only as long as the enemy continues to fight back. The same sort of selective reading is occasionally practiced by some non-Muslims regarding Qur'an 9:5, which is sometimes referred to as the "sword verse." The first part of the verse, which contains a call to kill unbelievers "where you find them," is cited as evidence of Islam's inherently violent nature and its intolerance toward non-Muslims. But these words are immediately followed in the second half of the verse by the command to let them go if they repent, pray, and pay alms, a section that is often ignored by those who seek to paint a negative picture of Islam. These passages provide examples of what is sometimes referred to as the *"jihād* of the sword," which permits the use of violence in order to spread or defend Islam. Most modern Muslim thinkers believe that this is no longer a legitimate way to spread Islam since the religion is now found in virtually every part of the earth and the circumstances of the Prophet's time no longer apply. Others, particularly extremists and radical Islamists, disagree and argue that the faith must be spread by any means necessary. Not surprisingly, there is more agreement on the use of force when Islam is under attack. But there is still some debate on this point since, as we will see, not all Muslims agree on what constitutes a legitimate attack.

These two sets of meanings for the Arabic root *jahada* in the Qur'an and other Islamic sources have given rise to a distinction between two types of *jihād*, one of a personal nature and the other more public and sometimes violent. They are mentioned in the *hadīth* at the beginning of this chapter—"We have returned from the lesser *jihād* to the greater *jihād*." According to tradition, Muhammad spoke these words after he and his followers had returned from a military campaign. The lesser *jihād* refers to the effort involved in trying to spread the faith and expand the community of believers. This "*jihād* of the sword" is limited in scope and duration and can sometimes involve warfare, especially in defense of the faith.

The greater *jihād*, on the other hand, is a duty incumbent upon all Muslims. It describes the daily effort one must exert to submit oneself fully to Allah's will and avoid the temptation to do evil. Unlike the *jihād* of the battlefield that the Prophet and his companions were able to leave behind, this is an ongoing struggle that must be waged every day of a person's life. It is sometimes called the "*jihād* of the heart" or the "*jihād* of the tongue," identifying the other means by which Muslims can attract other people to their religion. By leading good lives and speaking words of encouragement, they become models of Islamic piety and embodiments of their faith.

As its adjective suggests, the greater *jihād* plays a more important role in Islam and the lives of its adherents. When Muslims hear the term *jihād*, it is this meaning that is primary for them. This is not to deny that the word can have a more violent connotation that has permitted warfare and other acts of aggression. But non-Muslims should exercise caution by being aware of the range of meanings for the word *jihād* and not defining it too narrowly. They distort its sense if they simply give it the meaning "holy war," a term never found in the Qur'an that does not do justice to the complexity of the concept. Ironically, one of the Arabic words most familiar to people who do not speak the language is also one of the most misunderstood. For Muslims, the confrontation with the self, rather than the confrontation with the enemy, is the more important battle.

BIN LADEN'S *JIHĀD*

Perhaps the most notorious recent example of an attempt to call for a lesser *jihād* is that of Osama bin Laden (1957–2011), the mastermind behind the attacks on the United States on September 11, 2001. After his Saudi citizenship was revoked, bin Laden spent a good portion of the 1980s supporting the cause of the Afghans in their struggle against the Soviet Union. His vast personal wealth, a result of his family's construction business, gave him virtually unlimited resources to back the *mujāhidīn*, a group of Afghans and Muslims from other countries dedicated to overcoming the Soviet forces. The term *mujāhidīn* is also sometimes used in reference to other paramilitary groups that join forces under a militant Islamist ideology. The word's etymological connection to *jihād* is obvious, and it can be translated as "those who strive." It appears four times in the Qur'an in reference to those engaged in armed combat (4:95 [3x]; 47:31).

Once the Soviets were defeated, bin Laden offered to provide *mujāhidīn* protection for Saudi Arabia against Iraq during the Gulf War in 1991. The Saudis' rejection of his offer was a bitter pill for bin Laden to swallow, especially when they turned to the United States for help. The subsequent occupation of Saudi Arabia by US troops was interpreted by bin Laden as a betrayal by the Saudi regime, which he maintained had contaminated the Holy Land of Islam by allowing an infidel army within its borders, and was a further example of neocolonialism by a Western power whose only concern was the region's oil supply.

These events help to explain the origin and content of two documents issued by bin Laden in the years prior to the 2001 attacks. The first is the "Declaration of War against the Americans Occupying the Land of the Two Holy Places," which appeared in August 1996—a statement addressed to Muslims everywhere, particularly those in the Arab world. It is a lengthy document that speaks of the people of Islam as a target for the repeated aggression of the "Crusader-Zionist alliance," and it identifies the US occupation of Saudi soil as the most serious offense. Ibn Taymiyya, a medieval Muslim scholar who was mentioned in the previous chapter, is cited repeatedly to support the removal of non-Muslim forces from Muslim territory. The depth of bin Laden's rage at the American presence in Saudi Arabia is seen in his statement that, after belief, there is no more important duty for a Muslim than to push the American enemy out of the land of Islam.

The second document is titled "Jihād against Jews and Crusaders," a *fatwā* issued in February 1998 in the names of Osama bin Laden and four other radical Islamists, including his top lieutenant, Dr. Ayman al-Zawahiri. The statement begins with a listing of "three facts known to everyone": (1) for more than seven years, the United States has occupied Islam's Holy Land, controlled its leaders, and humiliated its citizens; (2) despite the great destruction they have brought upon the people of Iraq, the Crusader-Zionist alliance continues to wreak havoc in the area; (3) America's primary aim is to serve Israel by diverting attention away from the Jewish occupation of Jerusalem and the murder of Muslims there.

The document identifies these actions as a declaration of war on Allah, Muhammad, and Muslims, and it states that *jihād* is an individual duty of each Muslim if an enemy attempts to destroy a Muslim country. The *fatwā* itself then follows, parts of it providing a rationale for the events of September 2001:

The ruling to kill the Americans and their allies, civilians, and

military, is an individual duty for every Muslim who can do
it in any country in which it is possible to do it. This is to
be done in order to liberate the al-Aqsa Mosque and the holy
mosque from their grip, and in order for their armies to move
out of all the lands of Islam, defeated and unable to threaten any
Muslim. . . . We, with Allah's help, call on every Muslim who
believes in Allah and wishes to be rewarded to comply with
Allah's order to kill the Americans and plunder their money
wherever and whenever they find it. We also call on Muslim
'ulamā' [legal scholars], leaders, youth, and soldiers to launch a
raid on Satan's American troops and the devil's supporters allied
with them, and to displace those who are behind them so they
may learn a lesson.

The vast majority of Muslims believed that bin Laden's
fatwā had no merit since the criteria for calling a lesser *jihād*
had not been met in this case. The opposition to it became
more unified and vocal after the attacks that occurred in
New York, Washington, D.C., and Pennsylvania. Its critics
have identified several shortcomings in the *fatwā*. In the first
place, the Qur'an and other Islamic sources indicate that any
attack must be defensive in nature and the result of a direct
threat on Islam and/or its followers. It is true that many
Muslims have concerns about too much American presence
and influence in Islamic countries, and they also frequently
disagree with US policy in the Middle East and elsewhere.
But they recognize that this does not constitute the kind of
threat that warrants the response called for in bin Laden's
fatwā.

A second problem concerns the identity of the individual

issuing the *fatwā*. Bin Laden was not a trained legal scholar, and many have questioned his interpretation of the primary sources of Islam. In addition, a ruling of this sort cannot be promulgated by just anyone. Normally, the authority rests only with the recognized leader of a state or some other political entity, a role bin Laden did not enjoy.

Furthermore, the terrorist attacks in America violated one of the fundamental rules of engagement in Islam, since every effort must be made to avoid injury or death to innocent people, particularly children, women, and the elderly or infirm. Clearly, that precept was not followed in this case; and virtually all Muslims have concluded that what occurred in September 2001 was an example of murder, not lesser *jihād*.

An additional problem with bin Laden's 1998 *fatwā* is that he and his co-authors are guilty of the same type of selective reading of the Qur'an that was discussed earlier. The document quotes less than ten Qur'an passages, and it does so with a type of prooftexting that is meant to legitimate the authors' position and influence the readers' behavior. They cite the opening portion of 2:193, which reads, "Fight them until there is no more persecution, and religion is devoted to God." But the second half of the verse, which has a more tolerant and compassionate tone, is not included—"If they desist let there be no further hostility, except against transgressors." This message did not fit bin Laden's agenda, so only the half-verse that served his purposes was lifted out and inserted into the *fatwā*.

In both the documents mentioned above, as well as in other pronouncements he issued, bin Laden made reference to the longstanding conflict between the Israelis and the Palestinians. In his "Declaration of War against the Americans Occupying the Land of the Two Holy Places," he reminded his fellow Muslims of their duty. "Your brothers in Palestine and in the land of the two Holy Places are calling upon you for help to fight against their enemy and your enemy, the Americans and the Israelis."

Through statements like this, bin Laden attempted to garner support for his ideas by appealing to the strong sense of community that is basic to Muslim identity. If one part of the *ummah* is suffering and in need of help, those in other areas of the world should do what they can to assist them. Similarly, his references to the Israeli occupation of Jerusalem in the documents were meant to play on the emotions and loyalty of Muslims. As the third most holy city in the world for Islam, Jerusalem is a place that is highly revered by its followers. Calling attention to the plight of the Palestinian people and identifying other concerns that are shared by many Muslims around the world was a strategy by which bin Laden attempted to make his ideas palatable and acceptable to as wide an audience as possible.

On a related note, the Palestinian response to Israel should not be identified as an example of lesser *jihād*. This is the view of the Palestinians themselves, who refer to it as an *intifāḍah*, or uprising. The actions of certain individuals on behalf of the *intifāḍah*, like suicide bombers, are sometimes termed *jihād* by those who carry them out or by observers, but this is not an appropriate way to categorize the entire movement. The tensions between the two sides, which date back to the creation of the state of Israel in the late 1940s, are the result of a conglomeration of historical, social, political, and cultural factors. To define it in strictly theological terms by calling it a *jihād* would be to focus on the religious component to the exclusion of other equally important elements.

JIHĀD AND THE NON-MUSLIMS

The word *jihād* appears frequently in the media and public discourse, and in the wake of terrorist attacks much of this usage is in reference to lesser *jihād*. This is an understandable development, but it can lead to potential problems. Many non-Muslims are unaware of or misinformed about the true meaning of the term to begin with, and its frequent use in media reports might cause them to assume that the word is synonymous with violence done by Muslims.

A news story from a few years back illustrates this point. A Muslim student at Harvard University was selected by his classmates to deliver an address at commencement. The announcement of the title of his speech—"Of Faith and Citizenship: My American Jihad"—led to an uproar among students and other concerned parties who demanded that the speech explicitly condemn terrorist violence. The student changed the speech's title to "Of Faith and Citizenship" but did not alter its content which, ironically, criticized Muslims and non-Muslims who have misunderstood and abused the word *jihād*. The idea that the term *jihād* is offensive and somehow not appropriate for such an occasion is nothing but a knee-jerk reaction due to a lack of familiarity with its proper meaning and the roles it plays in Islam.

It is important for non-Muslims to appreciate the complexity of the concept *jihād* and not simply equate it with violence and bloodshed. Muslims are permitted to engage in war if they are under attack and the proper criteria are followed. At times, as in the case of Osama bin Laden, those criteria are ignored or disregarded and the resulting situation can have disastrous effects.

But there is also the other *jihād*, the greater *jihād* that defines the day-in, day-out struggle of every Muslim to remain true to the faith. This is a meaning that non-Muslims can more easily relate to and learn from. The presence of temptation and the possibility of falling short are not unique to Islam. Jews, Christians, and members of other faiths (as well as people who follow no religion) face the same challenges on a daily basis and, like Muslims, must at times put forth great effort to overcome them. This concept, which they sometimes misunderstand, is therefore a key component of the lives of non-Muslims who also must, in the words of the Prophet Muhammad, "return to the greater *jihād*." As strange as it might sound to some, each one of us is a *jihādī*.

QUESTIONS FOR DISCUSSION

1. Does the concept of *jihād* have any connection with other religious traditions you are familiar with? What are the main similarities and differences?

2. What are some of the primary sources for your understanding of what *jihād* means?
3. Do you think the term *jihād* should be avoided or replaced with another word because of the images and ideas associated with it?
4. What is your reaction to the idea of a "holy war"?
5. What relevance does the notion of greater *jihād* as the ongoing struggle to be a good person have for your own life?

Resources

BOOKS

Arjana, Sophia Rose. *Muslims in the Western Imagination* (Oxford: Oxford University Press, 2015). A study of how Muslims have been portrayed as monsters by Westerners through a survey of medieval, early modern, and modern literature, art, and film.

Armour, Rollin. *Islam, Christianity, and the West: A Troubled History* (Maryknoll, NY: Orbis Books, 2002). This book presents a clearly written account of the history of Christian perceptions of Islam. It covers the main figures and developments that have been influential in shaping how Christians view Muslims.

Esposito, John L. *Islam: The Straight Path* (New York: Oxford University Press, 2010). In its fourth edition, this book is an excellent general introduction to Islam. The author, director of Georgetown University's Center for Muslim-Christian Understanding, presents an overview of the fundamental elements of Islam and how the religion has evolved in different periods and contexts.

Esposito, John L. and Dalia Mogahed. *Who Speaks for Islam? What a Billion Muslims Really Think* (New York: Gallup Press, 2007). This book presents the findings of a survey of Muslims in more than thirty-five countries that was conducted between

2001 and 2007. It includes analysis of their views on politics, extremism, gender, and relations with non-Muslims.

Firestone, Reuven. *Jihad: The Origin of Holy War in Islam* (New York: Oxford University Press, 1999). This work offers a study of the concept of *jihād* (particularly lesser *jihād*) within the Islamic sources. It discusses the way the Qur'an, prophetic traditions, and biographies of Muhammad present the subject, and attempts to explain how it has come to take on the sense of "holy war."

Green, Todd H. *The Fear of Islam: An Introduction to Islamophobia in the West* (Minneapolis: Fortress Press, 2015). This work traces the history of Western fears of Islam and the various forms it takes in the modern world. It includes information culled from interviews with eight prominent Muslims and non-Muslims.

Kaltner, John. *Introducing the Qur'an: For Today's Reader* (Minneapolis: Fortress Press, 2011). An overview of how the Qur'an treats seven topics of interest for modern readers: the natural environment; the family; gender and sexuality; Muslim/ non-Muslim relations; *jihād*; violence and war; and death and the afterlife.

Nasr, Seyyed Hossein. *The Study Qur'an: A New Translation and Commentary* (San Francisco: HarperOne, 2015). An English translation of the Qur'an containing detailed notes on each verse that summarize how Muslim commentators have interpreted the text throughout history.

Siddiqui, Mona. *Christians, Muslims, and Jesus* (New Haven: Yale University Press, 2013). An exploration of the figure of Jesus in Muslim-Christian relations that focuses on key themes, including revelation, prophecy, salvation, sin, law, and redemption.

WEBSITES

http://acmcu.georgetown.edu/. Georgetown University's Prince

Alwaleed bin Talal Center for Muslim-Christian Understanding provides a website that contains a wealth of information related to Islam and Muslim-Christian relations.

http://islam.uga.edu/. A website maintained by Dr. Alan Godlas of the University of Georgia that includes resources related to Islam grouped under main headings. It contains excellent articles, images, and audio resources that cover a wide array of themes and issues.

http://www.cair.com/. The website of the Council on American-Islamic Relations provides information that enhances understanding of Islam, encourages dialogue, protects civil liberties, and builds coalitions.

http://kurzman.unc.edu/islamic-statements-against-terrorism/. Dr. Charles Kurzman of the University of North Carolina at Chapel Hill created this website that is a collection of various statements that Muslim individuals and groups have made since 9/11 that denounce terrorism in the name of Islam.

http://www.pewresearch.org/topics/muslims-and-islam/. This site contains reports and data on Islam and Muslims that summarize surveys that have been administered by the Pew Research Center.